WHERE THE MIND
MEETS THE BODY

WHERE

Type A, the Relaxation Response,

THE MIND

Psychoneuroimmunology, Biofeedback,

MEETS

Neuropeptides, Hypnosis, Imagery

THE BODY

*and the Search for the Mind's Effect
on Physical Health*

HARRIS DIENSTFREY

HarperCollins*Publishers*

FIRST EDITION
ISBN 0-06-016570-7
Library of Congress 90-55532

91 92 93 94 CC/HC 10 9 8 7 6 5 4 3 2 1

FOR JANE,
A TOKEN

Contents

CONTENTS

Can the
Mid Be in Charge?

What kind of mind moves the body? This somewhat airy question first came to me while I was working with an organization that helped disseminate scientific information about the mind's effects on health and disease. My main job was to edit a quarterly journal that reported on new findings and that generally tried to find a way to think about the whole odd issue of an intangible mind influencing the physical health of the brutely tangible body.

Most of the contributors to the journal were researchers and clinicians, and over the course of time, it became clear to me, as it would to most editors grappling with a poorly defined and sprawling subject, that there were many unconnected facets to the study of mind-body relationships. Some researchers examined whether situations that subjected people to out-of-the-ordinary pressures or demands, commonly called stress, could be associated with rates of ill health. Some researchers attempted to associate a particular disease with a certain emotional or behavioral pattern. Other researchers focused on bodily mechanisms that could serve to connect mental or emotional events to physiological processes. Still other researchers taught animals and sometimes humans to use certain kinds of mental activities to alter specific physiological reactions—blood pressure, for example, or an immune response.

My sense of how to put all these pieces together was dramatically changed by an article with the long and cumbersome title "Changing 'Unchangeable' Bodily Processes by (Hypnotic) Suggestions: A New Look at Hypnosis, Cognitions, Imagining, and the Mind-Body Problem." The article was written by a psychologist, Theodore X. Barber, who I later learned was a maverick in the field of hypnosis. Barber put parentheses around the word "hypnotic" in his title because he held that hypnosis was fundamentally no different from any other carefully presented suggestion.

Barber had assembled over 60 clinical studies in which people under hypnosis or suggestion succeeded in altering physiological processes of their bodies simply by imagining the changes or otherwise mentally directing their bodies to make the changes. A group of adolescent boys gave themselves a poison ivy–like rash as part of an experiment. People afflicted with medically untreatable skin diseases, from which some of the individuals had suffered all their lives, restored much of their disturbed skin to a normal condition. About 70 women increased the size of their breasts.

The article was a revelation to me. Here was example after example of people who were able to change internal bodily processes more or less by deliberate command. The people called for the changes, and the changes came. In virtually all the other mind-body studies I knew about, mind-induced physiological changes in animals or humans happened without the volition or intentions of the subjects. Rats that were restrained developed ulcers as a result of the frustration caused by the restraint; they did not intentionally seek to give themselves ulcers. People whose ill health seemed to be related to certain patterns of behavior did not engage in the behavior to become ill. In all such instances, which constitute the bulk of studies investigating the mind's influence on the body, activities of the mind or the emotions triggered physiological reactions automatically, as in a Rube Goldberg contraption that proceeds from step to step all on its own. In these cases, the mind in essence acted mindlessly.

When I spoke to people about what seemed to me the unique "mindful" character of the mind-body events in Barber's article, I rarely found anyone who thought that this difference was as intriguing and as exciting as I did. Everybody knew about such findings—they were familiar stuff—and to most people, they were just one more aspect of the mind-body scientific landscape. I was told in effect that Barber was interested in hypnosis and suggestion, that other people pursued other avenues of interest, and that eventually all the different studies would find their appropriate places in a full understanding of the mind's capacity to affect the health of the body.

But as my knowledge of mind-body studies increased, I came to another view. To my way of thinking, most mind-body investigators were not much interested in the mind part of the connection. Not only did they generally think that the difference between a commanding mind and a mind that operated in a knee-jerk fashion was a matter of little importance, but they were largely uninterested in distinguishing among the mental and emotional phenomena whose bodily effects they variously explored. Some researchers focused on emotions or stress, others focused on learning processes. Rare was the researcher who thought that these differences mattered, or who even noticed them. Individual scientists are always at pains to explain how their studies differ from the studies of everyone else, but mind-body investigators never seemed to use the particular aspects of "mind" that they were looking at to identify the distinctiveness of their work. It was a little as if literary critics went on about their business without a clear acknowledgment of the differences between poems and novels.

The more I thought about mind-body studies and the more I tried to sort out the possibilities of the mind affecting the health of the body, the more I found myself looking to the particular aspects of "mind" that one way or another led to physiological changes. This book is the result.

IN the following pages I examine seven investigations of the mind's effect on the body. The investigations represent different approaches to the study of mind and body. Together they display a rainbow-like array of "minds"—different kinds of mental and emotional phenomena as well as minds that react passively and minds that act directly—and they range widely over a broad geography of bodily conditions, processes, and structures.

With each investigation, I describe the experience or perception that initiated the inquiry, and then describe how the investigators often painstakingly built their insights into larger pictures of the mind's influence on the body. Many of these efforts are variously marked by courage, determination, ingenuity, and remarkable thoughtfulness, and although I look at the investigations from my own perspective, I have tried to do justice to their intrinsic merits and their drama.

All of the investigations are important, and all are illuminating. I consider several of them extraordinary achievements. But I make no claim that they constitute the seven most important explorations of mind and body. The future will have a hand in deciding what is "most important."

My aim is twofold. By focusing on the "mind" of each investigation and on the bodily feature that is being affected, I want to show the expansive scope of the mind's involvement with the body and ultimately with health and disease. Not just one aspect of the mind affects the body, but many aspects. Not just one area or property of the body can be affected, but many.

My second aim is broader and more argumentative. I want to make the case that only a mind that directly affects the body can be the basis for a medicine that fully enlists the mind to heal the body.

JUST as there are many "minds" in the study of mind and body, there are many meanings to the word "mind." "Mind" in the term "mind-body studies" or the phrase "the mind's influence on the body" generally refers to phenomena that are commonly labeled "subjective"—phenomena that lack physical dimensions, that are idiosyncratic to an individual and cannot be verified by anyone else or by physical measurement, that come from the "head" or the "heart." These phenomena include feelings, emotions, thoughts, opinions, attitudes, perspectives, and learning processes.

Most investigators of mind-body phenomena, as is probably clear by now, rarely talk of the mind at all, and if they do, they usually do not mean it. Either they are using the word as a gesture to common usage, or they mean by "mind" the brain and the central nervous system, the mechanisms an organism uses to process information from outside and within the body. Most mind-body investigators believe that the phenomena commonly associated with the mind—feelings, attitudes, learning processes, and so on—are in fact phenomena of the brain. In this perspective, "mind-body studies" is a misnomer that should be relabeled "brain-body studies."

For my own part, I will use the stiff phrase "emotional and mental phenomena," as I have once or twice already, to refer as simply as I can to the phenomena commonly associated with the mind and attributed to the brain by most mind-body investigators. I will also use the word "mind" and will use quotation marks to distinguish two meanings. I will put quotes around the word when I examine the kind of machine-like, mindless "mind" that is implied in most mind-body studies—the "mind" that operates without awareness or choice. I will bypass the quotes when I speak of a mind that acts on a body because a person wants it to. Such a mind seems to me to deserve to be called a mind.

These comments should reveal my own views. I believe that there is a mind and that a person can use the mind to act on the body and influence its physiology. Whether the mind is in the brain does not matter in this context. The mind is the entity that allows us to respond to the new and enables us to achieve new insights. The mind keeps us from endlessly repeating routine behavior. The mind is our tool for meeting the changing demands of life, which sometimes come in the form of pathogens.

No doubt I will stumble into usages of the word "mind" that I am not aware of. I apologize in advance for any confusion. To talk about mind-body is to enter a thicket of terminology—which may be one reason why most mind-body investigators, who have other things on what I can rightly call their minds, do not want to become entangled with the word and its meanings.

MIND-BODY studies are a source of controversy, and the whole idea that the mind, whatever it may be, could severely affect the health of the body is not warmly accepted by prominent portions of the medical community. The attack on mind-body studies that received the most attention in the medical research community appeared in 1985 in an editorial in the prestigious *New England Journal of Medicine.* The editorial declared that it was time to acknowledge "that our belief in disease as a direct reflection of mental state is largely folklore." The notion that an individual's mental state—a person's feelings, attitudes, emotional outlook—was a source of disease, the editorial went on, was especially hurtful to patients. "At a time when patients are already burdened by disease," it maintained, "they should not be further burdened by having to accept responsibility for the outcome."

The weakness of this argument will become clear in the course of the book. The editorial is talking about only one general feature of the "mind"—mental state. Even if the connection between mental state and disease is "largely" folklore—and the connection is hard to demonstrate—this says nothing about the connection between the body and other general features of the "mind," particularly the mind's capacity to learn.

But readers may also be interested to know that much the same sort of protect-the-patient argument was made almost exactly 100 years ago in a comparable attack on the very theory that now is taken to represent a clear limit to the mind's capacity to affect the body. In the closing decades of the 19th century, the advocates of the germ theory, led by the great French scientist Louis Pasteur, fought for their belief that individual diseases were each caused by individual microscopic entities. Today, this theory is regarded as the truth of infectious disease and the model for understanding all disease. The medical community generally presumes that the source of each definable illness is likely to be a single physical entity—if not a "germ," then a deficient gene or an improper amount of a chemical produced by the body—a view of disease that leaves the "mind" with very little to influence.

A century ago the medical community dismissed this view of disease. In 1884, when cholera epidemics menaced Europe and the United States, an editorial in the *Journal of the American Medical Association,* then as now a major medical research journal, took the announcement of the German scientist Robert Koch that he had identified the microbe that caused cholera as an occasion to condemn the idea of the germ theory. The "popular germ theories," the editorial declared, "greatly exaggerated by the newspaper press, are adding to the terror of all classes of people." The terror came from the fact that germs were microscopic, invisible to the normal eye, and so people felt helpless before them. They could be anywhere! The effect of the terror, maintained the editorial in a line of reasoning that would appeal to today's investigators of the mind's effects on the body, will be to "increase the destructive effects of the epidemic wherever it makes its appearance. For of all the predisposing causes of cholera, fear, dread, and mental trepidation are among the most efficient."

The following report on seven mind-body investigations should make clear that the level of health today would likely be higher if the medical community had retained a bit of its skepticism toward the germ theory and was more responsive to the capacity of the mind to move the physiology of the body.

WHERE THE MIND
MEETS THE BODY

CHAPTER 1

Type A and the Emotions That Can Lead to Heart Disease

SOMETIME in the early 1950s, Meyer Friedman and Ray Rosenman, cardiologists on the staff of the Harold Brunn Institute for Cardiovascular Research, decided that the steady clarification of the sources of heart disease—which killed more Americans than did any other disease—was leaving something out. The cardiologists did not doubt the research findings that high cholesterol levels, cigarette smoking, and lack of exercise each increased the risk of developing heart disease. But demographic data and their own experiences as cardiologists persuaded them that such risk factors, as they are called, could not be the whole story.

They knew, for example, that individual countries with similar diets and therefore roughly similar cholesterol levels could have as much as a fourfold difference in rates of heart disease. They also knew that heart disease rates had risen sharply in several industrial countries while the average intake of fat had stayed the same. Such evidence clearly did not fit the general finding that heart disease rose as cholesterol levels increased.

In their daily treatment of people with heart disease, Fried-

1

man and Rosenman also regularly saw people with a certain common emotional style, and the two cardiologists came to believe that this style was another contributing source of heart disease. That emotions are involved in heart disease is not a new thought. The lore of medicine is filled with anecdotes about people who became so overwrought or enraged that they keeled over dead from a heart attack. But Friedman and Rosenman set out to put their idea to the test of systematic research.

The result was the concept of Type A behavior, the first researched formulation that seemed to offer clear and solid evidence that feelings and emotions—which Friedman and Rosenman called a behavior pattern—could contribute to the development of disease. Friedman and Rosenman's crucial study found that men with the Type A behavior pattern—a composite of driving competitiveness, aggressiveness, and impatience and anger at the delays and frustrations of everyday experience—were twice as likely to develop heart disease as men without this behavior pattern (Type Bs, the two cardiologists dubbed them).

The Type A findings had a tremendous impact on the public and on the study of mind and body. To the public, the idea that aggressively competitive and ambitious behavior in the workplace could lead to heart disease seemed like an immediately recognizable truth. When Friedman and Rosenman wrote a book about their studies for the lay public, *Type A Behavior and Your Heart,* readers made it a best-seller, and the popular media were quickly filled with references to Type A. Comedians made jokes about it and magazines ran articles on how to get rid of it. With a sort of perverse pride, people would boast that they were Type As, meaning more that they worked too hard and were impatient with delays than that they were superior candidates for heart disease—though some implied that they were so competitive they would run the risk. (Since the end of the 19th century, Americans have boasted that the country's businessmen would make themselves ill by working too much.)

Type A became so much a part of American life and culture that the term is now regularly included in American dictionaries, the only concept from the study of mind and body to have achieved that status.

Among researchers, especially younger researchers, Friedman and Rosenman's achievement promised to open a new chapter in the study of mind and body. Connections between emotions and health had been notoriously difficult to document. A critical problem was characterizing and then quantifying emotions, which seemed inherently nebulous and subjective. By enfolding emotions, along with goals and attitudes, in the behavior through which they were expressed, Friedman and Rosenman seemed to show how to objectify the subjective.

The findings on Type A behavior led to a deluge of studies seeking to replicate and extend the findings and to gain a better understanding of the precise components that comprised the Type A behavior pattern. Then, unexpectedly, a few studies failed to find an association between Type A behavior and heart disease. The failures became more numerous and more serious. Type A behavior no longer seemed intimately involved in heart disease, and several researchers began to explore the possible impact on heart disease of other emotion-connected behavior, particularly hostility.

Today, apart from Friedman and his associates and supporters on one side and advocates of the "hostility hypothesis" on the other, no one knows quite what to make of the Type A behavior pattern and why it sometimes was associated with heart disease and sometimes was not. Is there still an unidentified aspect of Type A behavior that can explain both the positive and negative findings? Or are the positive findings a bizarre fluke that have nothing to do with Type A? Friedman and Rosenman have made emotion and heart disease a researchable issue, but their work has raised questions that so far have not been resolved.

When many people think of the mind's effect on the body, they think primarily of the effect of emotions. The story of Type A behavior illustrates the difficulties in attempting to document a connection between emotion (or a behavior pattern) and the body's health. It also suggests why the kind of "mind" that is usually implied in studies exploring the physical effects of emotion is an uncertain guide to the realm in which the mind meets the body.

Initial Data-Gathering

Friedman and Rosenman began what eventually would be an assault on the established understanding of heart disease—and indirectly the established understanding of medicine—cautiously, almost hesitantly.

In one study, they compared the fatty diets of well-to-do businessmen with the diets of the businessmen's wives. Men in the administrative levels of business represented a sizable percentage of the people who had heart attacks. Women from the middle and upper classes represented a small percentage. If cholesterol played an important part in heart disease, it seemed likely that the diets of the men would be much richer in fats than the diets of the women. The diets turned out to be roughly equivalent.

Strictly speaking, the result proved nothing. Maybe the men would not go on to have heart attacks. Maybe their previous diets had been fattier and they would have heart attacks. Maybe the men would have heart attacks because they did not exercise and their wives did. But for the cardiologists, the result strengthened their view that something other than cholesterol—maybe something that they saw in their offices—was a critical cause of heart disease.

In another study, Friedman and Rosenman asked 150 San Francisco businessmen to select from a list of approximately a dozen items the traits that characterized friends before they had had heart attacks. The cardiologists sent a similar request to 100 internists who treated heart problems, to identify the traits that the doctors thought characterized their patients before they had heart attacks. More than 70 percent of the businessmen and a majority of the internists picked "excessive competitive drive and meeting deadlines."

The Physiological Effects of "Deadline Pressure"

Friedman and Rosenman had a fairly good idea of the outlook, behavior, and emotions that they thought contributed to heart disease. Earlier observers, Rosenman noted, had often commented that people with heart disease were excessively strenuous, hard-driving, aggressive, and intensely goal-oriented. These traits were the same general characteristics that he and Friedman observed in their patients, particularly those under age 60. The patients were aggressive, ambitious, competitive, preoccupied with deadlines, and absorbed by work. As Rosenman saw them, they were engaged in "a relatively chronic and excessive struggle to obtain an unlimited number of things from the environment in the shortest period of time." Their struggle often brought them into conflict with "other persons or things in the same environment." To Friedman and Rosenman, the observations of the businessmen and internists who said that "meeting deadlines" characterized people who went on to have heart attacks, fit perfectly with their own observations.

The question now was, could something like "deadline pressure" affect physiology in such a way that it could contribute to heart disease? Friedman and Rosenman decided to study 40 accountants, to see what happened to their cholesterol levels and blood-clotting speeds (once thought to be an important element in clogging heart arteries) as the accountants approached the tax-filing deadline of April 15.

The two cardiologists observed the accountants for a six-month period, starting approximately three months before April 15 and ending approximately three months after. Every two weeks, Friedman and Rosenman obtained blood samples from the accountants and had the samples tested for cholesterol levels and blood-clotting speed. In January and February, the cholesterol levels and blood-clotting speeds were stable and in the normal ranges. In April, both shot up abruptly. In fact, the accountants' blood "began clotting at a dangerously accelerated rate." Then in May and June, the measures returned to the stable, normal levels of the pre-deadline period.

During this six-month period, the accountants did not substantially change the foods they ate or the amount of exercise they performed. The only major change was the pressure of meeting the April 15 deadline. As far as Friedman and Rosenman were concerned, the deadline pressure had clearly affected the physiology of the accountants and pointed them in the direction of the processes that lead to heart disease.

Other cardiologists, Friedman reports, were not much interested in the finding that a form of stress was associated with physiological changes linked to heart disease. When Rosenman presented the data at an annual meeting of the American Heart Association, there was "only a dead silence." Friedman thought of Lincoln's Gettysburg Address. "We felt very much as Lincoln must have felt at Gettysburg when a similar silence followed the delivery of his address."

Defining and Comparing Type As and Type Bs

Friedman and Rosenman could now say that the process of meeting a deadline had the sort of physiological effects that were involved in heart disease. But they could not say that a pattern of behavior--a routine way of dealing with the world--could have the same effects. To investigate this question, they needed to compare the cholesterol levels and blood-clotting speeds of the aggressive and competitive people whom the cardiologists would come to call Type As and of the relaxed and unassertive people they would call Type Bs.

A key problem in the effort to show that an emotion or an emotion-laden behavior pattern is associated with the development of a disease is the seemingly technical matter of defining the emotion and then measuring it. How does one define an emotion so that it can be measured? If the emotion is defined in terms of behavior, how can one be sure that the behavior captures all the aspects of the emotion that may affect the development of disease? The problem, endemic in the study of the possible effect of personality on disease, would come to haunt Type A studies.

The two cardiologists began by itemizing what they then saw as the six major characteristics of their Type A patients. First, Type A people had an intense drive to achieve self-determined goals that were often poorly defined—for example, wanting to be the "best" in a line of work without being able to say what "best" meant. Second, Type A people had a profound propensity to compete. Third, they had a persistent desire for recognition and advancement. Fourth, they had a habitual tendency to do their work faster and faster. Fifth, they were extremely alert, mentally and physically. Finally, they regularly involved themselves in a series of multiple activities that all had deadlines.

Type Bs were just the opposite. As Friedman and Rosenman saw them, they displayed a "relative absence of drive,

7

ambition, sense of urgency, desire to compete, or involvement in deadlines."

The two cardiologists then asked businessmen to identify associates who displayed the Type A or B behavior pattern. This was 1957, and the selections were all men.

In interviews with the men, Friedman and Rosenman obtained information about the men's eating and exercise habits and about their prior illnesses. The information about prior illness was to contain an important, unanticipated surprise.

The cardiologists found that the men picked as Type As or Type Bs tended to describe themselves differently and that they had distinctly different "expressive" styles. The Type A men tended to consider themselves ambitious and competitive and often felt that a day did not have enough hours for them to accomplish their goals. They displayed "excessively rapid body movements, tense facial and body musculature, explosive conversational intonations, hand or teeth clenching, excessive unconscious gesturing, and a general air of impatience." Type Bs, on the other hand, "sat relaxedly, moved slowly and calmly, exhibited no muscular tension, spoke slowly, rarely indulged in tense gestures, exhibited no impatience."

Using their observations and the self-descriptions of the men, Friedman and Rosenman classified 83 men as Type As and 83 men as Type Bs. A number of them had some but not all of the traits of their particular types and the cardiologists labeled these men "incomplete" Type As or Bs.

Friedman and Rosenman had their Type As and their Type Bs. Did the distinction make any physiological difference?

It did for cholesterol levels. The average cholesterol levels of the Type A group were markedly higher than the levels of the Type B group. The figures on blood clotting were weaker. The differences between Type As and Type Bs were statistically significant—could be attributed to more than chance—only for the "complete" Type As or Bs.

But to Friedman and Rosenman this was a minor setback, especially in light of the entirely unanticipated finding that emerged from the analysis of the prior illnesses of the study's subjects. From the information collected in the interviews, the cardiologists learned that the percentage of Type A men who already had heart disease was fully seven times greater than the percentage of Type B men who had heart disease. Twenty-three of the Type A men, 28 percent, had had a "coronary episode." But only three of the Type B men, 4 percent, had had such an episode. (The three men, moreover, were "incomplete" Type Bs—they had elements of Type A behavior. Apparently, even a small amount of Type A behavior could be deleterious to one's health.)

The finding was so remarkable because the men had been declared Type A or B only on the basis of their behavior. They had not been picked as Type A or B because of their history of heart disease. Yet the behavioral designations had revealed extraordinarily different rates of heart disease. It surely seemed that Type A behavior was a "marker" for heart disease and that Friedman and Rosenman's list of Type A traits correctly characterized crucial aspects of the Type A behavior pattern.

But the finding had a limitation. There was no way to tell from the data whether Type A behavior had led to the coronary episodes or, as remote as the possibility seemed, whether the coronary episodes had somehow led to Type A behavior. To prove that the behavior came first, a study needed to start with healthy Type As and Bs and then follow them until it was statistically clear that Type A men had a greater likelihood of heart disease than Type B men.

Such a prospective study, as it is called, demands a large number of subjects, lasts years, and necessarily costs a lot of money. It is not the kind of study that individual researchers can mount easily.

During the time that Friedman and Rosenman were conducting their first comparative study of Type As and Bs,

Friedman visited the National Heart Institute (which is now the National Heart, Lung and Blood Institute) to find out why the Institute had twice rejected a proposal from the cardiologists for a grant to conduct a prospective study of Type A behavior and its influence on heart disease. An official of the Institute told him that the problem was the psychiatrists who reviewed the proposal. The cardiologists at this stage in their work were using the term "emotional stress" to describe the nonphysiological factor that they believed contributed to heart disease, and the psychiatrists, the official explained, "apparently doubted that two cardiologists and a biochemist [Sanford O. Byers, a colleague who worked with Friedman and Rosenman] were equipped to study emotional matters, and refused funding." The official suggested that they change the wording of their proposal. "I believe you fellows are describing a behavior pattern, something that you have actually witnessed," he told Friedman. "Why don't you just label it Type A behavior pattern? That shouldn't upset the psychiatrists."

The cardiologists made the change in the third version of the proposal. They received their grant and in 1960 and 1961, with additional funds from a variety of foundations and heart associations and with two other teams of researchers (one would focus on cholesterol level and heart disease, the other on blood-clotting speed and heart disease), Friedman and Rosenman began the prospective research project—the Western Collaborative Group Study—that in a dozen years would make Type A a household term.

The Western Collaborative Group Study

The Western Collaborative Group Study consisted of approximately 3,100 volunteers, all businessmen from the San Francisco–Oakland and Los Angeles areas, all free of heart disease. Friedman and Rosenman had refined their method for determining who was a Type A and who was not. They had devised an interview of about 20 questions. It became known as the "structured interview," and for many years it was the preferred method for determining whether or not a person was a Type A.

Some of the questions asked people to describe their feelings when they encountered everyday frustrations, such as waiting in a line; other questions asked people how their close friends might describe them—as competitive, for example, or ambitious. Several questions were patently obvious and were asked in a deliberately slow and hesitant manner. Type A people, Friedman and Rosenman believed, tended to snap out the answer before an interviewer could finish the question. In general, the way in which a person answered was as important as what a person said. In the cardiologists' view, Type A people tended to respond harshly and explosively, Type B people calmly and quietly.

After listening to audio tapes of all the individual interviews, Friedman and Rosenman determined that the participants of the study were about equally divided between Type As and Bs. Their classification was based on both the content and the style of a person's answers. The two elements could sometimes war with each other, and then an element of interpretation was necessary. A person might say, "Any friend of mine would be absolutely crazy to think that I was unusually aggressive," but to Friedman and Rosenman, the formulation and the delivery rather than the literal meaning expressed the person's behavioral type.

The Western Collaborative Group Study lasted approximately 8½ years. (Some of the participants were tracked for 9 years, some for 8, depending on when they started.) At the end of the project, the findings on Type A behavior seemed starkly clear: Healthy Type A men were twice as likely to develop heart disease as healthy Type B men. During the study, 257 men (out of 3,154) developed heart disease. Of this number, 178 were Type A and 79, less than half as many, were Type B. The numbers might appear small, but statistically speaking their meaning was not in doubt.

The two-to-one ratio between Type A and Type B held for all the measures of heart disease that the study had tracked. Twice as many Type A as Type B men had regular heart attacks, twice as many had "silent" myocardial infarctions (episodes that occur without pain but leave signs that are revealed by electrocardiograms), twice as many had angina (severe heart pain), and twice as many died from their heart attacks.

The data also demonstrated that the effect of Type A behavior could not be accounted for by other risk factors. Smoking had an effect, cholesterol had an effect, and Type A behavior similarly had its own effect. Furthermore, when Type A was added to smoking or to any other risk factor or combination of risk factors, the total rate of heart disease was higher than it would be without Type A. This would not have been the case had Type As somehow been an artifact consisting of the other factors. The data testified that Type A behavior was real and that it made heart disease more likely.

Type A: Taken to Heart

With the Western Collaborative Group Study, whose results became known in the early 1970s, Friedman and Rosenman succeeded in introducing a new understanding of heart disease into medical research. The importance given their findings is illustrated by the response of a large government-funded heart study that was already in progress. Starting in 1971, the Multiple Risk Factor Intervention Trial—whose acronym, MRFIT, is pronounced "Mr. Fit" (only men were in the study)—sought to determine whether reductions in the known risk factors of cholesterol levels, cigarette smoking,

12

and high blood pressure would lead to reductions in the rates of heart disease. Then, in 1973, in acknowledgment of Friedman and Rosenman's finding about a nonphysiological risk factor for heart disease, the steering committee of MRFIT decided to open the investigation to "a prospective study of the behavior pattern hypothesis." The whole subject and methodology of Type A was so new, but seemed so important, that MRFIT even engaged Ray Rosenman to teach its interviewing personnel how to conduct and interpret the structured interview.

In 1974, Friedman and Rosenman published *Type A Behavior and Your Heart* and provided the American public with a new item to add to the list of self-defining labels that had gained popular currency over the last two decades: the lonely crowd, the organization man, exurbanites, and now, Type A.

Partly in response to the enormous interest in Type A, public and professional, the National Heart and Lung Institute funded a conference in 1977 to examine the accumulating data on what it generically called coronary-prone behavior. The conference recommended that a special panel consider the Type A material by itself. Four years later, the panel, somewhat like a diagnostic licensing board, declared that Type A behavior was indeed a risk factor for heart disease and reported that the degree of risk was approximately the same as the risk created by high blood pressure, high cholesterol, and smoking.

In some 20 years, Friedman and Rosenman had shown that an aspect of "mind" could increase the likelihood of a disease that medicine had previously understood to be the result of only physiological factors. With heart disease, the cardiologists wrote, "an error in spirit" could lead to "a failure in matter."

Amidst the triumph, there was little reason to notice that the descriptions of Type A were not altogether stable. The description in *Type A Behavior and Your Heart* contained many of the usual elements: an "excessive competitive drive,

aggressiveness, impatience, and a harrying sense of time urgency." But it also contained two elements that had not had
much, if any, notice before: "a deep-seated insecurity" and "a
free-floating but well-rationalized form of hostility." If anyone cared to think about it, the odd plasticity of the concept
of Type A—like a beanbag slowly shifting its weight—might
suggest that the behavior that could break the heart was not
yet fully understood.

The Recurrent Coronary Preventive Project

In 1977, Friedman (whose partnership with Rosenman had
ended sometime after the publication of *Type A Behavior and
Your Heart*) and a team of colleagues began a new research
study, the Recurrent Coronary Preventive Project. Friedman
wanted to demonstrate for Type A what MRFIT wanted to
demonstrate for cholesterol, smoking, and high blood pressure: that a reduction in a risk factor for heart disease would
lower the rate of heart disease. Friedman's problem was
more complicated than the task facing the MRFIT study.
Before he could show that a reduction in Type A behavior
would bring about a reduction in the rate of heart disease, he
first had to determine that Type A behavior could be reduced.

The word "recurrent" in the title of the study referred to the
fact that the participants would be people who had already
had heart attacks. Statistically speaking, such people would
have another attack before healthy people would have their
first attacks, a difference that would cut down on the length
(and cost) of the study. People who had had heart attacks
would also be more likely to try and change their behavior
than people who had not had such an experience.

In about a year's time, in August 1978, Friedman and his
colleagues had recruited approximately 1,000 participants.
All were Type As, a number were women (a relative rarity in

14

heart studies), all had had at least one heart attack, and none were smokers. Friedman regarded the last characteristic as something of a concession to critics of Type A. "We did not relish the prospect of spending thousands of hours trying to change Type A behavior—and in doing so reduce the cardiac recurrent rate—only to have our colleagues attribute the reduction to a decline in smoking."

The participants were organized into three groups. One group of about 425 people was given standard cardiac counseling. They were told about healthy and unhealthy diets, safe and dangerous physical activities, the operations of the cardiovascular system, and how it changed when something in it went wrong. A second group of about 425 people—the key group of the study—were given standard cardiac counseling and also special counseling intended to reduce their Type A behavior. The third group of about 150 people served as a control. These people were under a doctor's care in a routine way and received no special information about heart disease.

If Friedman and his colleagues were right, the Type A behavior of the group with special Type A counseling would drop more sharply than would the Type A behavior of the other groups (whose members might change their behavior in the course of coming to terms with the experience of a heart attack), and the result would be a lower rate of recurrent heart attacks.

The Recurrent Coronary Preventive Project was scheduled to last 5 years. The picture was clear by the end of 3, and the project was concluded in a total of 4½ years. First of all, the people in the special Type A counseling group reduced their Type A behavior by almost 30 percent, far more than in either of the other groups. More important, the reduction in Type A behavior was accompanied by a reduction in recurrent heart attacks. The rate of recurrent heart attacks in the special counseling group was roughly half the rate of the other groups. In the special counseling group, the rate was 3 percent; in the standard cardiac counseling group, 6.6 percent; in the control group, 5.7 percent (numerically but not statistically different from the 6.6 percent of the standard counseling group).

As far as Friedman and his colleagues were concerned, they had shown that Type A was not just associated with heart disease but was a causal source of it. In *Treating Type A Behavior and Your Heart,* the report on the project (published in 1984) that Friedman wrote with Diane Ulmer, the study's field director, Friedman and Ulmer assert that Type A—the emphasis is theirs—is *"the first of all the commonly accepted coronary risk factors to be directly demonstrated as bearing not just associational but causal relevance to clinical coronary heart disease."*

But the odd thing about the Type A of the Recurrent Coronary Preventive Project is that it is not the Type A of the Western Collaborative Group Study. In the earlier study, Type A behavior is clearly related to the American workplace. The traits of Type A behavior are competitiveness, aggressiveness, impatience, and ambition, all presumably encouraged by the work environment. In the Recurrent Coronary Preventive Project, the self and a wounded psyche have replaced the workplace, which is nowhere in sight. Friedman and his colleagues focus on three traits: "a continuously harrying sense of time," "easily aroused free-floating hostility," and feelings of insecurity, which, according to Friedman, are the source of the other two traits and can be traced back to an individual's childhood.

Friedman himself makes no note of the change in perspective, but it is clear that the beanbag of Type A behavior was still shifting its shape.

The findings of Friedman's treatment program for reducing Type A behavior and with it the rate of heart disease did not attract large public interest (although patients continue to take the program, which Friedman offers in California) and attracted virtually no clinical interest. For the research community, the critical news about Type A was not the findings of the treatment program but the reports that an increasing number of other studies had failed to find an association between Type A behavior and heart disease. The problems with the concept of Type A were beginning to emerge.

Type A Detractors

Some of the studies that failed to find an association between Type A and heart disease had been trying to replicate Friedman and Rosenman's original findings with people other than businessmen. Some studies attempted to refine the association between Type A and heart disease. Some studies had large populations, some had small. Some had a broad focus, some a narrow. They did not all have equal weight, but none of them could link Type A to heart disease. Together they added up to a large problem: Was the Type A association with heart disease real or not? A few observers who never cared much for Type A, or for the general effort to show that the mind had the capacity to influence the health of the body, asked a larger question: Could physical illness really have a source in what Friedman and Rosenman, in an unusual flourish of rhetoric, called "spirit"?

To Friedman and the supporters of Type A, the first failures to find an association between Type A behavior and heart disease could be explained by the fact that the researchers had used a pencil-and-paper questionnaire to identify Type A behavior. Such a questionnaire was intrinsically flawed. Type A behavior after all was *behavior* and had to be judged as such. Were the subjects brusque and tense? Did they interrupt the interviewers? This kind of information was not available from a pencil-and-paper questionnaire. Type A behavior had to be studied through the structured interview that Friedman and Rosenman had developed to characterize the style

17

as well as the content of an individual's comments.

Then came the report of the MRFIT study, which had used the structured interview and had even hired Ray Rosenman to teach the study's interviewers how to use it. MRFIT also failed to find an association between Type A and heart disease.

A swirl of controversy surrounds the MRFIT Type A interviews. Rosenman himself, although no longer a partisan defender of the Type A concept, has criticized the interviewing as "sadly deficient." He "didn't select the interviewers," he told a reporter, and he "refused to train some of them, because they were so incompetent." It has also been charged that the interviews were often conducted at a pace that did not allow Type A people to vent their impatience and hostility. Seemingly in anticipation of such criticisms, the report of the study noted that "at no time during the period of intake did Dr. Rosenman . . . indicate that any interviewer was conducting interviews in an unacceptable manner."

The controversy concerning the interviews did little to minimize the serious doubts that MRFIT cast over Type A. MRFIT was a sign that the failure to find an association between Type A behavior and heart disease could not automatically be explained by a technical failure in methodology. Perhaps there was something substantively wrong with concept of Type A behavior.

In 1985, the year the MRFIT findings appeared (the results had become known several years earlier), a study in the *New England Journal of Medicine* looked at the association over time between Type A behavior and mortality, and found none. Type As who had recovered from heart attacks died from heart disease no sooner and in no greater numbers than Type Bs who had recovered from heart attacks. The behavior that presumably increased the occurrence of heart disease had no apparent effect on mortality, so could it really be increasing heart disease? (The finding could also be taken to mean that there was little value, so far as longevity was concerned, in the kind of treatment program that Friedman and his colleagues tested in the Recurrent Coronary Preventive Project.)

The crowning insult came three years later, in another study in the *New England Journal of Medicine.* This study went back to the subjects of Friedman and Rosenman's breakthrough investigation of Type A behavior, the Western Collaborative Group Study, which found that men with Type A behavior were twice as likely to develop heart disease as men with Type B behavior and twice as likely to die from it. At the end of the study, 257 men had developed heart disease and two thirds of them, 178, were Type As; 50 men had died of heart attacks and, again, two thirds of them, 34, were Type As. The new study wanted to know what had happened to the remaining people who had developed heart disease. These people had been classified as Type A or B by Friedman and Rosenman, so there could be no dispute about the methodological correctness of the classification.

According to the Type A understanding of heart disease and the pattern of findings in the Western Collaborative Group Study, one would expect that among the men with heart disease, those with Type A behavior would continue to die at a higher rate than those with Type B behavior. The new study found just the reverse. It was the men with Type B behavior—the people with a "relative absence of drive, ambition, sense of urgency, desire to compete, or involvement in deadlines"—died at a higher rate.

The new data had made a full turn. Not only did they fail to demonstrate an increased risk of dying from heart disease for men with Type A behavior, but they found an increased risk for men with Type B behavior.

Whatever the full meaning of these data, they indicated that the leading presumptions of the Type A perspective on heart disease—simply and unstatistically put, that Type A behavior led to heart disease and Type B behavior did not— were no longer clearly demonstrable.

19

Perhaps because the reversal was so unexpected and appeared to strike so deeply into the concept of Type A behavior (Friedman tends to describe such studies as research that substitutes "statistical quasi-expertise for clinical acumen"), no one took the time to savor the fact that the findings still pointed to a connection between behavior and heart disease—only now it was the relaxed people who were at greater risk. Could it be that a style of, say, easygoing placidity is at times deadly for one's heart?

Hostility and Heart Disease

As confidence in Type A declined, interest grew in studies that linked other behavioral constructs to heart disease. The most prominent of these studies, primarily the work of Redford Williams, a leading figure in the field of behavioral medicine, argues that hostility is the behavioral source of heart disease. Friedman, in his later work, has called hostility an important part of Type A behavior. Williams says that hostility is the only behavior that contributes to heart disease, that the behavior of competition and ambition, originally associated with Type A, has nothing to do with it. The shift from competitiveness to hostility appeals to Williams, he explains in his book *The Trusting Heart,* published in 1989. "Surely it would do more good for humankind to show that being hostile is bad for health than to show that being quick and ambitious is harmful."

Williams has made the case for hostility as Friedman and Rosenman made the case for Type A behavior, in a series of increasingly larger steps. In one study (with James Blumenthal), he has shown that while both hostility and Type A behavior were associated with severe blockages in one or more coronary arteries (arteriosclerosis), the association of hostility was larger. Patients with Type A behavior were 1⅓

20

times more likely to have severe blockages than were patients without Type A behavior, but patients with high hostility scores were 1½ times more likely to have severe blockages than were patients with low hostility scores. In statistical terms, the difference between 1⅓ and 1½ is important.

In a prospective study (with Grant Dahlstrom, the principal investigator, and John Barefoot), Williams has shown that among a group of 255 physicians who graduated from the University of North Carolina's medical school in the years 1954 to 1959, the physicians who had registered high hostility scores on certain school tests were four to five times more likely to have coronary episodes in the 20-year period after their graduation than were the physicians who had registered low hostility scores.

One of the strongest pieces of evidence supporting the hostility hypothesis comes from another reexamination of Friedman and Rosenman's Western Collaborative Group Study. Researchers took information obtained from the structured interviews in that study and divided it into 12 components that had been found to be elements in the Type A behavior pattern. Some components were concerned with the way people said things—loudly, for example, or competitively. Some components were concerned with traits of character— ambitiousness, for example, or hostility. When the researchers examined the association of each component to the development of heart disease, they found that only hostility had a strong predictive impact on the development of heart disease. Although other components of Type A added to the influence of hostility, the difference was not statistically significant. According to this study, the very heart, the only true core, of Type A is hostility.

But already two studies have failed to find an association between hostility and heart disease. Williams argues that the problem is the people being studied. In one instance, he maintains, the subjects had good reason to hide their hostility: They were applying for medical school and were trying to put "their best foot forward." In the other instance, the participants (middle-aged Minnesota businessmen) probably were not hostile to begin with or at least not enough of them were sufficiently hostile to have a statistical effect, as a group with only a few high-cholesterol people might not reveal a connection between cholesterol levels and heart disease.

Williams may be right about these studies, but the story of hostility and heart disease is beginning to sound like the story of Type A behavior revisited. The critical point is that since no one has explained *why* some Type A studies found an association with heart disease and some did not (even if hostility is, in essence, Type A, this does not explain why the Type A findings are so inconsistent), there is no strong reason to believe that the bad times that have befallen Type A will not also befall the hostility hypothesis. Williams (and others, of course) believe that the problem with the Type A concept lies in its content: It is simply tapping into the wrong behavior. But it is possible to argue that the problem is the nature of the concept and the kind of "mind" that is implicit in both it and the concept of hostility.

The Type A "Mind"

The "mind" that the concepts of Type A and hostility both presume—and that is presumed by virtually all the concepts that researchers currently use to link disease to feelings— works on the body like this: A person has a certain set of feelings (attitudes, goals, emotions, beliefs, self-perceptions) that leads the person to react to certain circumstances in the same way, again and again. The feelings have an internal physiological effect: An increase in blood pressure, a rise in cholesterol levels, the weakening of a particular immune re- action. As the reactions continue, so do the physiological effects. Over time, the effects build up until, finally, by the sheer weight of things, the body gives in—the heart breaks or the cells begin to multiply without restraint or the immune system, which should protect the body against alien invaders, treats the body as if it were the alien invader.

This is the acid rain or rusting bridge view of mind and body. A douse of acid rain has little effect, but a continuing downfall brings disaster. A little rust makes no difference, but a deepening accumulation pulls the bridge apart. In such a process, the end effect is not foreseen. It comes about through forces that take place on their own.

What this view of mind and body leaves out, of course, is the "mindful" mind, the mind that regularly gives a particular meaning to a person's behavior and experience. Consider one of the central (initial) traits of Type A—aggressive competitiveness. Aggressive competitiveness can clearly mean different things to different people. Some people are aggressively competitive because it is a sport-like activity that gives them pleasure. Some people are aggressively competitive because they are filled with envy. Some people are aggressively competitive because they want to prove their superiority over other people.

With a concept like Type A—with any concept that presumes that an emotion or a behavioral pattern has a single inevitable physiological effect on the body—such differences do not matter. People who are aggressively competitive, whatever the underlying reason, all run the same fundamental risk for developing heart disease.

But this makes no sense. It is not reasonable that the playful competitor, the envious competitor, and the domineering competitor all experience the same physiological effects from competition. For the playful competitor, competition is joyful. If "positive" emotions sustain health, then the playful competitor may stay healthy by being competitive. For the envious and domineering competitors, competition likely involves ultimately unsatisfiable strivings; further, since winning is not always possible, it will involve losses that bring self-pity to the envious competitor and demoralization to the domineering competitor. The consequences for the body cannot be the same as the consequences of playful competition, and may even be different between envious and domineering competitors.

As concepts, Type A and hostility are abstractions. Their reality—how they actually operate in the lives of people—can come only from the people who experience them, from the meaning-assigning minds of the people who experience them. From this perspective, it is no surprise that some Type A studies have found an association between behavior and heart disease and some have not: Some studies arguably have examined people who attach meanings to competition (or hostility) that presumably can lead to heart disease; some studies have not.

From this perspective, it is possible to understand why a sudden terrible event can precipitate a heart attack: The meaning attributed to the event is too devastating. (Why the result should be a heart attack rather than another physical expression of illness is, of course, a critical question.)

From this perspective, it is even possible to imagine that easygoing, relaxed, and placid behavior might lead to heart disease—if such behavior was given the "right" meaning.

A concept like Type A treats the mind and the body as if they were machines operating without intention. But if intention and meaning—acts of the mind—are what moves people, how can a "mind-less" concept like Type A (or hostility) be a consistent guide to the mind's effect on the body?

CHAPTER 2

Herbert Benson
and the Balm of the Relaxation
Response

WHILE Meyer Friedman and Ray Rosenman were on the West Coast investigating a behavioral source of heart disease, another cardiologist researcher, Herbert Benson, was on the East Coast, at Harvard, investigating the impact of emotional and behavioral pressures on high blood pressure, a condition associated with heart disease. One can easily imagine the West Coast cardiologists getting together with the East Coast cardiologist to discuss their mutual interests and their shadowy status in a medical community that generally believed that only something as concrete as the body could affect physical health and that gave little credence to medical researchers who thought that the mind mattered too.

An interchange between the investigators on both coasts is even easier to imagine when it turned out that there could be an important point of connection in their research. Friedman and Rosenman found that certain internally generated emotional pressures increased the likelihood of heart disease. Benson (with another researcher, R. Keith Wallace) found that a self-mobilized technique of mental concentration, derived from meditative practices, had the property of calming many physiological activities of the body. Might not Benson's calming technique be helpful to people whose competitive drive pushed their bodies into high gear and so increased their risk for heart disease?

But the investigators on opposite sides of the country paid no attention to each other; they might as well have been on separate planets. Each line of inquiry went its own way, and each made its own very different contribution.

Despite their possible interconnections, the investigations had important differences. Friedman and Rosenman aimed at disclosing the contribution of emotion (wrapped in a behavioral guise) to the development of a particular disease. Benson discovered that a mental technique—a twist of the mind, so to speak—benefited the body by tamping down a range of physiological processes. In Friedman and Rosenman's research emotion takes its toll over time, unknown to the person being affected. In Benson's research, the act of concentration produces its effect in a matter of minutes and is used deliberately because the person wants these effects.

The differences can be summarized this way: With Friedman and Rosenman, the mind, through emotion, works secretly in the dark of the body to create illness. With Benson, the mind, through its capacity to direct its attention, is intentionally manipulated to bring to the body a physiological calm. Friedman and Rosenman's work is about the "mind" expressed in emotion; Benson's work is about the "mind" involved in an act of concentration. Benson's work—like whole areas of mind-body research—has nothing to do with emotion.

Benson named the mental technique he uncovered and the effects it produces the relaxation response, which, next to Type A, is the second-best-known phenomenon to emerge from the contemporary effort to understand the mind's effect on the body. Among portions of the American public—the people who are interested in self-help or self-realization or

26

who go to psychotherapists—the relaxation response is probably as common as aspirin or vitamin C.

The story of Benson's relaxation response makes clear that there is more than one way to mind the health of the body.

Hypertension Studies

Benson's initial work on high blood pressure, or hypertension, in the late 1950s into the 1960s parallels the approach that Friedman and Rosenman took in their studies of Type A. He wanted to explore, as did they, whether emotion in one form or another could induce disease. In his case, he wanted to know whether emotions, stimulated by behavioral demands and punishments, could increase blood pressure and lead to hypertension.

Benson and various colleagues pursued this concern in studies with animals, usually monkeys. Typically, the monkeys were taught to perform a task on demand—such as pressing a lever 30 times in 30 seconds—and were punished with a mild electric shock to their tails whenever they failed. As this was going on, the researchers tracked the monkeys' blood pressure.

In studies with titles such as "Behaviorally Induced Hypertension in the Squirrel Monkey" and "Arterial Hypertension in the Squirrel Monkey During Behavioral Experiments," Benson and his colleagues demonstrated that they could take monkeys with normal blood pressures and make them hypertensive by putting them through training trials of demands and punishments. It was reasonable to speculate that a comparable pattern of demands and punishments—in the workplace, for example—could make humans hypertensive too.

Benson also began to explore the use of the mind to treat hypertension. The logic was simple. If an activity of the mind,

27

in the form of reactions to behavioral demands and punishments, could lead to an increase in blood pressure and ultimately to hypertension, perhaps an activity of the mind could succeed in lowering blood pressure and conceivably even provide a treatment for hypertension.

At this point Benson's work took an unacknowledged shift in focus. In the behavioral experiments on increasing blood pressure, Benson focused on emotion and the body. In the research on lowering blood pressure, he focused on what can be called mental techniques and the body.

Benson and his colleagues tried to lower blood pressure using biofeedback techniques. In biofeedback, an individual (or an animal) is attached to a machine that reports back information on a selected physiological activity (such as heart rate or blood pressure) and indicates when the activity is proceeding at an unacceptable rate or level (the animal usually receives a shock, the human usually stops receiving a light or sound signal). The subject then tries to bring the activity back to an acceptable rate or level and, in the case of the animal, stop the shock, or in the case of a person, resume the signal. To do this, the subject somehow, through trial and error, manipulates its inner response. The exact process of manipulation is mysterious, even to the people who successfully use the technique to gain a new control over an internal physiological activity.

But however it is done, the new control is learned. Biofeedback is a technique by which a subject masters an inner process through trial-and-error learning. It is not a technique that uses emotion—unceasing demands or repeated punishments—to increase the level of a physiological response. Benson paid no attention to the distinction between learning and emotional pressure, but he now drew on a different kind of "mind" than the one operating in the earlier studies.

In one biofeedback study, Benson and his colleagues found that people with hypertension were able to use biofeedback to lower their blood pressure a small amount. The drop was

28

statistically significant, but in practical terms the change was minimal.

Transcendental Meditation

Around 1968, as Benson tells the story, while he was working with monkeys and biofeedback, he was visited by several practitioners of transcendental meditation, or TM, a meditative technique that at the time had become fashionable among celebrities in the entertainment world. (Followers of TM included Mia Farrow and several of the Beatles.)

The TM people told Benson that they believed they could lower their blood pressure with their meditative technique, and they wanted Benson to test them. He said no, he was not interested. It is possible that the request made him uncomfortable. He was a young assistant professor at the Harvard Medical School, and fooling around with a trendy meditative technique had clear pitfalls.

For some reason, the TM practitioners asked again, and this time, for some reason, he agreed to test them. "I felt there was little to lose in a preliminary investigation," he recalled. There was also something to gain. He already knew that biofeedback could bring about a small reduction in blood pressure. But biofeedback was cumbersome and costly. Meditation was something that presumably anyone could do, and if it could lower blood pressure, it had clear practical advantages over biofeedback.

Transcendental meditation teaches a simple meditative technique that centers on the use of a word or phrase, called a mantra, and aims to bring about a state of inner peace. Every TM practitioner receives an individual mantra from a TM instructor, presumably because of its spiritual significance to the person. The mantra could be anything: "the light in the sky," "peace on earth," "nature," "fulfillment."

To meditate, a person sits in a comfortable position with closed eyes and silently repeats the mantra for about 20 minutes. The steady concentration on the mantra allows the person to "let go" of the swirl of thoughts, wishes, fears, and hopes that surges through the mind when it is attempting to be quiet. If the thoughts take over, the person simply returns to the mantra. Throughout the process, the mantra remains uppermost, and the person becomes detached from the buzzing turmoil of the responses to everyday life. TM practitioners meditate in this way several times a day, and with practice, they can achieve a sustaining calm.

The TM people who came to Benson argued that the calm induced by this form of meditation had a physiological base. Not only did meditators "feel" calm; in terms of their physiology they were calm. One aspect of this calmness, they believed, was a lowered blood pressure during meditation.

Benson teamed up with another researcher, R. Keith Wallace, to study the physiological effects of TM and to test in particular whether or not it lowered blood pressure. Wallace had been studying these issues at the University of California as part of his work for a Ph.D. in physiology. The approach was straightforward and matter-of-fact. Benson at Harvard and Wallace at the University of California each took a group of TM practitioners—together they had 36 men and women, 17 to 44 years old, who had been practicing TM for an average of 2 years each—and measured a number of physiological conditions 20 minutes before and after meditation, when the subjects would just sit quietly, and during a 20- to 30-minute meditation. If meditating had physiological effects that were different from sitting quietly, the measurements during the meditation session would be different and presumably lower than the measurements before and after.

The two researchers examined several changeable physiological conditions in addition to blood pressure. If meditation "quieted" blood pressure, it conceivably could quiet other conditions as well. Benson and Wallace measured heart and breathing rates, oxygen consumption (the less a body works, the less oxygen it metabolizes), amounts of blood lactate (a chemical substance that is produced by metabolism and that had been implicated in anxiety attacks), and alpha brain waves (which were associated with feelings of calm). A physiologically quieter body should have lower heart and breathing rates and lower amounts of blood lactate, and it should consume less oxygen and display alpha brain waves, as well as have lower blood pressure.

The results of the research showed that Benson and Wallace were right about everything except the blood pressure. It stayed the same before, during, and after meditation, but all the other conditions became quieter during meditation and then, afterwards, returned to the more active status that had been evident in the premeditation period. It was clear that TM effected a widespread calming of the body that was distinctly different from the physiological conditions that existed when a person sat quietly.

Benson and Wallace also noted that the calming was different from the physiological effects of sleep. During sleep, oxygen consumption drops about 8 percent below a person's consumption while awake, and drops gradually, over five to six hours. During meditation, oxygen consumption dropped 10 to 20 percent in a matter of minutes. During sleep, the alpha waves apparent during meditation were rarely present.

The Relaxation Response

Benson and Wallace read the results with excitement. The unchanging levels of blood pressure needed an explanation, but taking the results as a whole, it seemed to them that they had found an innate and integrated response of the body that was inducted by an activity of the mind (or brain).

They contrasted the response to the well-known phenomenon called the fight-or-flight response, which had been un-covered in 1914 by the great Harvard physiologist Walter Cannon (who did his research, Benson is pleased to tell audi-ences, in the same laboratory in which Benson studied the TM practitioners). Cannon found that the body produced an apparently integrated set of changes in response to danger or alarm. The heart rate went up, the breathing rate went up, metabolism rose, blood pressure rose, and blood rushed to the muscles. All these changes prepared the body for action—for "fight or flight," in Cannon's famous phrase. Not all of Benson and Wallace's findings were exact opposites of Can-non's. Most obviously, in Cannon's research blood pressure went up; in Benson and Wallace's research it stayed the same. But the basic lines of contrast were clear. What Benson and Wallace had found, they wrote, "looks very much like a coun-terpart of the fight-or-flight reaction."

The two researchers dubbed the meditation-induced physi-ological reaction a "wakeful, hypometabolic state." "Hypo" means "lower than normal." They had discovered a wakeful state of lower than normal metabolism.

In an article in *Scientific American,* "The Physiology of Meditation," they examined the health implications of their findings. The hypometabolic state, they wrote, represents "quiescence rather than hyperactivation of the sympathetic nervous system"—the part of the nervous system that mobil-izes the body for action and produces the changes observed by Cannon—and "may indicate a guidepost to better health."

Cannon had speculated that if the sympathetic nervous system, in response to perceived danger or threat, shifted too often into high gear, the excessive wear and tear might be a source of physical illness. Cannon's speculation has had a profound influence on much scientific thinking about the mind's possible effects on the body. It underlies the presump-tion that "stress" or a behavior pattern like Type A can bring the body to illness through the persistent repetition of a small deleterious physiological effect.

32

Benson and Wallace were guessing that perhaps the hypometabolic state could prevent the excessive mobilization of the sympathetic nervous system—and thus could be a source of good health. But before the two researchers began exploring this possibility, they had a parting of the ways. As Benson describes the rift, they fell out because they disagreed on whether or not transcendental meditation was essential to inducing the "wakeful, hypometabolic state." Wallace was a practitioner and advocate of TM and, according to Benson, "felt there was something unique about the techniques of transcendental meditation that caused the changes." Benson did not. He thought that "the key physical changes could be elicited regardless of any particular meditation technique."

The break was complete by October 1972. In that month, Benson spoke about his research before a group of psychiatrists and carefully made the point that many meditative, religious, and relaxation techniques could induce the physiological changes that he and Wallace had identified among the practitioners of TM. In fact, Benson maintained, meditative and religious practices and relaxation techniques that created a sense of well-being did so precisely because they induced such physiological changes.

In his talk, Benson called these changes by the name that has now become famous—the relaxation response. With this shift, the wakeful, hypometabolic state that was the relaxation response became, in effect, Benson's property.

Benson told his audience that the physiological changes of the relaxation response depend on a combination of four elements: a quiet environment, a comfortable position, a passive attitude, and what he calls a mental device. A person needs to be in an undisturbed and relaxing setting (the quiet environment and comfortable position), needs to focus on a sound or word or phrase (the mental device), and needs to let any thoughts that may come to mind "pass through" (the passive attitude). Anyone who does this for 10 to 20 minutes, "passively" concentrating on the mental device, usually by silently repeating it in rhythm with one's breathing, will induce the physiological changes of the relaxation response.

The four elements of the response, Benson claimed, could be found in many meditative and relaxation techniques, from yoga to certain forms of hypnosis, and even more significantly, in the meditative traditions of all the major religions. With the scientific method, Benson argued, he had pulled free a common set of elements by which people of all times and places have brought their bodies to a state of calm (and in some traditions, to a new state of spiritual awareness). He had identified the phenomenon in and of itself—a universal phenomenon—and detached it from the myriad contexts in which it had been embedded.

The Relaxation Response as Treatment

Benson (with Wallace) had shown that an act of focused and steady concentration would bring about a set of calming physiological changes. But could such changes be used to treat specific physical disorders?

Starting in the early 1970s, Benson conducted a number of small studies in which he used the relaxation response to treat various disorders such as headaches, arrhythmias (irregular heartbeats), and, most notably, high blood pressure, the problem that had led him to test the TM practitioners in the first place. He did not take any of these studies to a definitive conclusion. A fair example is the investigation in which he again examined whether meditation—this time, in the neutral form of the relaxation response—could lower blood pressure.

For some time Benson had surmised that the reason the meditators in his original studies with Wallace did not succeed in lowering their blood pressure was because they already had lowered it as much as they could through meditation. All the men and women had been TM practitioners for an average of two years. It was quite conceivable that meditation—the relaxation response now—could lower blood pressure only in beginning meditators.

Benson and several colleagues gathered 30 hypertensive people who were new applicants to TM—so new that they had not yet been given their mantras. Benson taught them the simple technique of focusing on a word (he told them to use the word "one"), had them meditate twice a day, and for six weeks tracked the levels of their blood pressure.

They went down. The subjects who meditated regularly succeeded in reducing their blood pressure to normal levels. The people with the highest pressure had the largest reductions, and the more a person meditated, the lower the pressure would fall.

Benson also found that if people stopped meditating, their blood pressure would begin to rise. Among a few subjects who stopped meditating fairly quickly, blood pressure levels resumed their original high measures.

Benson and his colleagues were cautious, almost reluctant, in making any claims for their study. Instead of pressing the findings to suggest specific further steps for exploring the use of the relaxation response as a possible treatment for high blood pressure, they emphasized the broad proposition that behavioral factors in general could contribute to hypertension and its treatment. The data, they concluded, "support the hypothesis that behavioral factors may play an important role in the development of hypertension, since hypertension in the present experiment was modified by a behavioral alteration." As to the therapeutic value of the relaxation response, it remains "to be established in the various types of hypertension and hypertensive disease."

Was meditation the equivalent of a drug for high blood pressure, which needed to be taken regularly to have an effect? Was it possible that meditation over time could change the physiology of the body and establish a permanently low level of blood pressure? Benson did not explore these questions in clinical studies. In terms of research, he has left the treatment value of the relaxation response an issue "to be established."

Around the mid-1970s Benson began to emphasize the general capacity of the relaxation response to calm the body and moderate or relieve the effects attributed to stress—fatigue, shortness of temper, sleeplessness. In 1974, he wrote an article for the *Harvard Business Review*, "Your Innate Asset for Combating Stress." His focus was on the relaxation response as a tool for calming down rather than a method for treating physical disorders.

Perhaps encouraged by the public interest in stress and by the best-selling success in 1974 of Friedman and Rosenman's *Type A Behavior and Your Heart*, Benson wrote *The Relaxation Response*, which was published in 1975. He offered the relaxation response as something of an all-purpose behavioral treatment for what he now escalated into the "overstress" of contemporary life. He downplayed the use of the relaxation response as a treatment for specific medical maladies. He discussed hypertension as something of an adjunct to stress—one of the most serious consequences, he suggests, of "overstress." His main point is the proposition that the relaxation response can counter "some of the harmful psychological and physiologic effects of our society."

With *The Relaxation Response*, the mental technique of meditation, as Benson outlined it, entered the public domain and the behavioral sciences as a method for dealing with the perturbations of the psyche rather than the body. The book achieved the same order of popularity as *Type A and Your Heart* and today exerts a broad interest among both the public and clinical therapists. In 1986 a sampling of psychotherapists identified *The Relaxation Response* as the self-help book that they were most likely to recommend to patients.

In the years since the publication of *The Relaxation Response*, clinical studies have shown that various relaxation techniques—the relaxation response is one among several—are moderately helpful in treating assorted conditions that include chronic pain, insomnia, headaches, and hypertension. No relaxation technique is the preferred treatment for any physical condition.

At the same time, various relaxation techniques, including the relaxation response, are used in many clinical situations to reduce tension, anxiety, and fear and to relieve and sometimes eliminate the physiological consequences that can accompany such feelings—nausea, muscle strain, pain, and loss of appetite. Essentially, the relaxation response, like other relaxation techniques, deals with physical symptoms that are clearly the expression of psychological turmoil.

Benson has written two more books about the relaxation response for the general public. In *Beyond the Relaxation Response,* published in 1979, he claims that the response will have more profound effects if people do it using words or phrases that evoke their deepest beliefs. ("The Lord is my Shepherd" is one of the many possibilities that he lists.) In *Your Maximum Mind,* published in 1985, he claims that after experiencing the relaxation response, people have a heightened capacity to change—to set new directions, drop old habits, develop new beliefs. Whether these claims are true is hard to say. Benson offers little in the way of support. But in either case, they are basically claims about the psychological rather than the physical benefits that flow from the relaxation response.

In practical terms, the contribution of the relaxation response lies primarily in the psychological domain. By secularizing meditation, Benson has made available to many Americans a mental technique that they can use to help themselves maintain a sense of calm self-possession, and he has given to therapists and psychologically oriented doctors a mental technique they can use to help patients who are suffering from anxiety and stressful agitation.

Benson and Other Mind-Body Phenomena

One factor that appears to have constrained Benson from pursuing more systematically the possible physiological consequences of the relaxation response is his inclination to doubt that anything other than the response is involved when an act of concentration seems to affect bodily processes. This attitude is evident in two episodes in which Benson examined exotic mind-body practices.

In the late 1970s, Benson and a team of researchers visited Upper Dharmsala, in India, to study claims that Tibetan Buddhist monks who practiced a devotional meditative practice called *gTum-mo* Yoga could appreciably raise the temperature of their bodies in the course of their meditation. With *gTum-mo* Yoga, monks sought "bliss," and one element of the process was to burn out "false perceptions of reality" with an "inner heat."

Benson and his team had three monks as subjects. The monks lived in "unheated, uninsulated stone huts," and each monk had been practicing *gTum-mo* Yoga daily for more than six years. While the monks meditated for Benson and his team, recording devices registered the temperature of their toes and fingers. In all three cases, Benson found that the temperatures increased substantially and for no other observable reason than the meditational practice.

The pattern of increases varied. One monk raised his finger temperature more than he raised his toe temperature—13 degrees (Fahrenheit) for his fingers, 7 degrees for his toes. The other two monks raised their toe temperatures more than their finger temperatures. One of these monks raised his finger temperature 9 degrees and his toe temperature nearly 13 degrees. The other monk had a smaller temperature increase in his fingers—something less than 6½ degrees—but the increase in his toe temperature was the largest rise of the study: 15 degrees.

Benson describes this episode in *Beyond the Relaxation Response,* in which he argues that the relaxation response can achieve deep effects if its practitioners use words or phrases that reflect their most serious beliefs. He maintains that the temperature increases of the monks is a vivid demonstration of his proposition. It is presumably the relaxation response combined with the monks' firmly held beliefs--or faith, as Benson likes to call it--that produced the temperature changes.

This is clearly a stingy interpretation of the phenomenon that Benson has observed. If the relaxation response plus a deep belief could achieve such a temperature increase, why was its occurrence such an out-of-the-ordinary event? Why was it that the monks who could produce such increases had been practicing *gTum-mo* Yoga for at least six years? Did their daily practice deepen their deep beliefs? And what exactly were they practicing? In *Your Maximum Mind,* Benson mentions in passing that the monks "mentally follow an image of a bodily energy called 'prana,' which is supposed to ignite an intense 'inner heat.' " Could one source of the temperature increases be imagery, an altogether different phenomenon than the relaxation response? However one views these events, they cannot be fully explained by Benson's proposition that they illustrate the power of the relaxation response plus faith. But this is where Benson is comfortable stopping.

Benson shows a similar disposition to overlook or discount phenomena that cannot be pinned to the relaxation response in an episode described in *Encounters with Qi* (1986), a book by one of Benson's former students, David Eisenberg. Eisenberg was the first American medical exchange student to go to the People's Republic of China where, in 1979 and 1980, he had the opportunity to observe so-called Qi masters. These men claimed to be able to exert an extraordinary degree of control over their energy—Qi, pronounced "chee"—which in traditional Chinese medicine and thought is said to sustain the body. Some Qi masters even claimed that they could externalize their Qi and move objects with it. Once Eisenberg saw a Qi master move a lamp and rotate a dart apparently with his Qi and certainly without touching them. Eisenberg was amazed. "Either I had been tricked or this was my first exposure to forces that Western science had not yet defined."

In 1983, Eisenberg returned to China with Benson, who was leading a research team to study Qi. Among the activities arranged by the Chinese hosts was a demonstration of "external Qi." The demonstration was held in an auditorium-like space in a Shanghai hospital. A young man, with his eyes closed, stood in the center of the room. Zhou, the Qi master, was off to one side, and as he gestured with his hands, the young man "responded" with corresponding movements of his body. Presumably Zhou was using his Qi to move the young man. Zhou then repeated the demonstration with a young woman. To Eisenberg, each of the young people had the motions of a marionette. The movements between master and subject were "so perfectly synchronized, it was impossible to say who was directing whom."

As Eisenberg tells the story, Benson stepped forward and asked if he might be a subject. Could the Qi master use his Qi to make Benson move, as the master had used his Qi to make the young people move? Zhou said that he could. This is Eisenberg's account of the episode:

> Benson stood in the middle of the large room, hands at his side, head slightly bowed, and feet together. Benson remained motionless, closed his eyes, and performed his own relaxation exercise. Zhou approached him cautiously, then aimed his arm at the Harvard professor's midsection. Benson appeared very relaxed, almost in a trance. Then he began to move. He swayed a bit from side to side, lost his footing, and tripped. He did not fall, but was clearly off balance. Zhou's arm tracked Benson's every movement, just as it had tracked those of the young girl and the young boy.

Once again, it was impossible to know who was leading whom. Benson then began to twist his hips, first to the right, then to the left. He swiveled 180 degrees with awkward jerks. Benson smiled an uninterpretable smile. Zhou smiled in response, but Benson, whose eyes were closed, could not see this. After five minutes of bizarre motion, Zhou stopped the exercise, placed his right hand on Benson's neck, massaged it, and performed what he called a "removal of excess of Qi." Benson opened his eyes, shook his head, and sat down to address the audience.

Benson explained that he was still not persuaded. He acknowledged that he felt "physical pressure seemingly coming from Zhou," but he said that he had moved voluntarily, "in an effort to resist Zhou's actions and test Zhou's strength." He claimed that "he had initiated all of his own movements and was not convinced that Zhou could move him in any direction against his own will."

Benson's remarks are ambiguous. He says he felt physical pressure and that he moved to resist and test Zhou but that he had initiated all of his actions, and so he still doubted that Zhou had the ability to use Qi to move a person against his own will. In Benson's formulation, the issue of external Qi becomes an issue of willpower rather than an issue of whether external Qi exists. Since Benson chose to move on his own accord, as he sees it, then the pressure he felt cannot be a demonstration of external Qi.

Clearly, something is awry here. ("The fact that Benson had any sensation of pressure from Zhou," Eisenberg notes without comment, "was interesting.") Is it too harsh an assessment to say that Benson might have been more open to the possibility of external Qi had this phenomenon been more easily accommodated to the effects of the relaxation response?

The Relaxation Response "Mind"

Benson's disinclination to press harder on the physiological events that he has already connected to the relaxation response may be compounded by a property of the relaxation response itself, a property of the kind of "mind" it embodies. A person who uses the relaxation response obviously uses it deliberately. In this sense, inducing the physiological effects of the response is a clear choice, in contrast to the process of inducing the physiological effects of the Type A behavior pattern—which, to repeat, happen because they happen and not because the Type A person wants them to happen.

But in another sense, the effects of the relaxation response, like the effects of Type A behavior, also happen at a remove from the person, as the appearance of electric light happens at a remove from the person who flips a light switch. The person who moves the switch to "on" wants the light that (usually) follows, but it is the mechanisms triggered by the movement of the switch that bring the light. The person is not triggering the light directly. The person cannot bypass the switch and still bring the light.

The operation of the relaxation response is similar. A person using the response wants the physiological and psychological effects that it produces, but to get them the person presumably needs to flip on the switch of the response.

In these terms, the "mind" implied by the relaxation response, like the "mind" implied by the Type A behavior pattern, is "mindless." It is not a mind of awareness. It does not move the body in a certain way because a person directs it to move the body in this way. It moves the body as it does because of its own inherent mechanisms that, apparently, are closed off to the direct intervention of an active and willful mind.

The Tibetan monks and the Qi master—if, for the moment, these examples can be taken at face value—both use minds

42

that appear to be in more or less direct contact with the body. The monks, it seems, call up an image of heat to increase the temperature of their bodies, and the temperatures go up. The Qi master goes directly to the energy within himself and externalizes it and then uses it to move people and objects.

It may be that the physiological effects of the relaxation response are limited because they are not the product of a "mindful" mind. Perhaps only a mind that is in direct touch with the body can move it deeply.

CHAPTER 3

Neal Miller,
the Dumb Autonomic Nervous
System, and Biofeedback

IN 1961, one of the country's premier experimental psychologists, Neal Miller, gave a lecture at the New York Academy of Sciences. With a few technical remarks about an issue that he thought needed to be studied, he set the stage for a remarkable series of experiments demonstrating that a whole system of bodily responses presumed to be beyond the influence of the mind (Miller would say brain) in fact were not. The issue that concerned Miller involved the responses of the autonomic nervous system. The autonomic nervous system gets its name from the fact that it regulates, entirely on its own and, it seems, innately, a complex of life-sustaining inner bodily processes collectively called visceral responses. These responses include heart rate, breathing, and blood flow. Unlike practically everyone else in the scientific community, Miller believed that the individual responses of the autonomic nervous system were entirely trainable—as trainable as the responses of the other major part of the nervous system, the somatic nervous system, the primary instrument through which an organism learns the repertoire of physical skills that enables it to move through the world.

The somatic nervous system controls the skeletal muscles. It is built for learning. The self-regulating autonomic nervous system, on the other hand, basically repeats the same activities again and again (although it must keep adjusting its responses swiftly and precisely to the ceaselessly changing inner conditions of the body) and in a sense never learns anything: It seems to have come into being knowing how to do what it does.

At the time that Miller gave his talk, the prevailing view of a "dumb" and fundamentally untrainable autonomic nervous system and a "smart" and infinitely adaptable somatic nervous system was related to the contrasting accomplishments of the two most prominent methods of getting an organism to learn new behavior—Pavlovian conditioning, also called classical conditioning, and trial-and-error learning, also called instrumental learning or instrumental conditioning.

Pavlovian conditioning works with the visceral responses of the autonomic nervous system. An existing visceral response is "connected" to a stimulus that has no intrinsic association with the response. In Pavlovian language, a natural, unconditioned stimulus is replaced by a conditioned stimulus.

Pavlov's famous experiment in which he taught a dog to salivate at the sound of a bell is the classic example. The dog already knew how to salivate, and when it naturally salivated at the appearance of food, it was simply engaging in an unconditioned response. Pavlov created a conditioned response by establishing an association between food and the sound of a bell. He rang a bell whenever the dog received food, and after he did this a sufficient number of times, the dog came to regard the unrelated entities of bell and food as a unit, and when the bell rang, the dog salivated. Pavlov had succeeded in teaching the dog to do an old trick in a new setting.

Trial-and-error or instrumental learning works altogether differently. It starts with any outward bit of behavior—learned behavior controlled by the somatic nervous system—

and through a series of rewards and punishments changes the old behavior to the new desired behavior. During lectures on instrumental learning, B. F. Skinner, its most famous practitioner, would rapidly teach a pigeon to do a figure eight or any other "reasonable" activity that the audience called for. In instrumental learning, a dog or pigeon (or human) does not simply learn to do an old trick in a new setting. It learns a completely new trick.

The enormous range of behavior that instrumental conditioning seemed capable of eliciting through the responses of the somatic nervous system, and the relatively narrow range of changes that Pavlovian conditioning seemed capable of achieving through the visceral responses of the autonomic nervous system, fed the idea that the learning capacities of the somatic nervous system were infinitely superior to those of the autonomic nervous system. Like Pavlov's dog, the autonomic nervous system seemingly could only learn to change the venue of a response. It could not control the response itself.

Miller thought otherwise. "We know," he told his professional audience in 1961, "that responses of the skeletal muscles innervated by the somatic nervous system are subject to instrumental learning. Many people believe, however, that visceral responses innervated by the autonomic nervous system are not subject to instrumental learning." It seemed to him "entirely possible that this apparent dichotomy is not the result of a basic difference in the fundamental properties of these two branches of the nervous system but, instead, is the result of the way in which . . . these systems are related to the environment under the normal conditions of life."

He meant that the responses of the somatic nervous system take place in the external world while the responses of the autonomic nervous system take place within the space of the body. When a person learning to drive steps on the gas instead of the clutch, the mistake is obvious and can be properly "punished." But if a person's blood pressure regularly

47

moves to a higher level in a certain situation, there is no way to do anything about it because there is no way to know about it.

For Miller, the challenge was clear. He believed that if visceral responses could be made "visible," it would be possible to apply instrumental learning to control and modify them. This possibility, he noted, had serious implications for the treatment of disorders that were thought to be psychosomatic, such as high blood pressure, an irregular heartbeat, and various gastrointestinal problems. Psychosomatic disorders invariably involved the visceral responses of the autonomic nervous system. If it turned out that visceral responses could be altered by instrumental conditioning, it could be that the disorders had been created by instrumental conditioning in first place. If the disorders in fact had been learned, they could be unlearned.

In the next decade, Miller would show that a system of the body thought to be impervious to the control of the mind was brightly responsive to it. One result of his work was the new field of biofeedback.

The First Animal Experiments

Miller, who at the time headed a research laboratory at Yale, faced great technical and methodological difficulties. He had to devise equipment that somehow would make it possible to "see" the inner visceral responses. He needed to figure out how to reward or punish an animal for making the right or wrong change in a response and how to do it quickly enough for the animal to associate the reward or punishment with the response.

He also had problems with personnel. Miller was an eminent figure, the head of a well-known lab at a famous university. Graduate students were honored to work with him to

earn their Ph.D.s. But few students could see any hope of success in his astounding idea that it was possible to train the visceral responses. "The belief that it is impossible for the stupid autonomic nervous system to exhibit the more sophisticated instrumental learning was so strong, it was extremely hard for me to get any students . . . to work seriously on the problem. I almost always ended up by letting them work on something they did not think was so preposterous."

Even assistants who were paid and not concerned about getting a Ph.D. approached the task with little conviction. "Their attempts were so half-hearted that it soon became more economical to let them work on some other problem which they could attack with greater faith and enthusiasm."

Finally, several students were willing to give Miller's idea a chance and to take the risk that if the idea was wrong, they would have to start all over on new Ph.D.s. The effort to train the autonomic nervous system began.

In his choice of animal subjects and the response he would attempt to train, Miller began as Pavlov had begun, with the salivation of dogs. Miller wanted to condition dogs to increase or decrease the amount of their salivation. Working with a student (Alfred Carmona), Miller used thirsty dogs as his subjects. Water was their reward, lack of water their punishment. Miller rewarded one group of dogs with water whenever they spontaneously salivated at a faster than usual rate, and another group whenever they spontaneously salivated at a slower than usual rate.

After 40 days, with a 45-minute training session each day, the rates changed up and down. The dogs that received water for salivating at a faster rate had generally increased their rate of salivation, and the dogs that received water for salivating at a slower rate had generally decreased their rate of salivation.

It was conceivable that water might trigger an innate response in regard to salivation, but if that were true, the rates would have changed in only one direction. An innate response could not make salivation rates go both up and down. It was clear that Miller and Carmona had instrumentally trained the salivation rates of their dogs.

What was not indisputably clear was whether they had done it through the autonomic nervous system. There was the possibility that the dogs, eager for water, had called on certain voluntary movements—panting or chewing—to change the salivation rates. Maybe Miller had only demonstrated once again the capabilities of the smart somatic nervous system.

Miller reasoned that the best way to rule out the use of the somatic nervous system was to paralyze it. It was possible that even when an animal was paralyzed, it might somehow call upon the voluntary movements that it controlled, but the chance was small. If Miller could train the automatic responses of paralyzed animals, his case would be powerfully strengthened.

Miller settled upon curare to paralyze the animals, and another of his students, Jay Trowill, spent three years maneuvering his way through the problems of trying to teach curarized rats to change their heart rates, some up, some down. Trowill first had to devise a machine that would record the rats' heart rates. Since curare paralyzes the respiratory system (which is why curare can kill), Trowill had to make a little breathing machine to keep the rats alive. (The machine included a respiratory mask that fit over the rodents' faces.) He also had to solve the technical problem of how much curare to use. Too much affected the heart rate; too little would not paralyze the rats long enough to train them.

On top of all this, he and Miller had to figure out how to reward a paralyzed rat. "There are not very many ways," Miller declared in deadpan understatement. He and Trowill decided to use electricity to stimulate an area in the brains of the rats known to provide pleasurable sensations. Trowill had to develop this piece of equipment too.

At one point, Miller despaired that he had sent the young

man down a dead-end alley. But Trowill, Miller was to write, stuck to his guns with "great ingenuity, courage, and persistence." After three years of machine building, problem solving, and, when everything was in place, response training, he succeeded. Stimulating a "pleasure center" in the brain, Trowill taught one group of paralyzed, machine-breathing rats to increase their heart rates and another group to decrease their rates.

The paralysis of the rats made it impossible for anyone to argue that any obvious overt voluntary behavior was the source of these changes. The case for visceral learning—for the educability of the stupid autonomic nervous system—had taken a large leap forward. At the same time, with Trowill's help, Miller had developed an experimental technique that would enable him to investigate the phenomenon in great depth.

Miller publicly presented Trowill's findings in 1967, at the Annual Meeting of the Pavlovian Society of North America. One member of the audience was James J. Lynch, who would become well-known as the author of *The Broken Heart,* a book about loneliness and heart disease published in 1977, and who is now a professor of psychology and Co-Director of the Psychophysiological Clinic and Laboratory at the University of Maryland School of Medicine. According to Lynch, the data were close to unbelievable. "The specificity and precision of the control seemed so remarkable that it almost appeared to defy well-established physical laws of hydraulics, let alone defy previously long-held beliefs in physiology!"

Refining, Verifying, and Expanding the Studies

One aspect of Trowill's results disappointed Miller: the relatively small average rate of change, about 5 percent in either direction. In instrumental conditioning of the somatic nervous system, much larger changes were possible. Could large changes be achieved with the autonomic nervous system too?

Working with another student, Leo V. DiCara, who became Miller's primary partner in the studies to follow, Miller refined his methods. The key to the change was a conditioning technique called "shaping." In the standard conditioning technique, all changes in a desired direction are rewarded. In shaping, the reward is used to encourage systematically increased levels of change. At first the animal is always rewarded for changes in the right direction. But as soon as the animal achieves a level of change and has accommodated itself to it, the reward is withheld until the animal moves on to an incrementally higher level of change. The process then starts all over again. In principle, the process can continue indefinitely, or until it reaches a bodily limit.

With shaping, Miller and DiCara succeeded in teaching curarized, electrically rewarded rats to increase or decrease their heart rates by an average of 20 percent. Miller's vision of an adaptable and instrumentally responsive autonomic nervous system seemed to be unfolding with powerful rapidity.

The two researchers now moved along several lines of investigation. They wanted to develop the parallels between the learning capacities of the somatic and autonomic nervous systems, and they wanted to strengthen their findings, both for themselves and for a scientific community that would need to be convinced that the established view of the autonomic nervous system—a view that had existed for decades—was simply wrong.

One line of investigation dealt with the technical possibility that the results in training heart rates were somehow a product of the way the change was achieved—that is, by a reward delivered via the brain. Perhaps there was an undiscovered inherent connection between the pleasurable stimulation of the brain and the ability to control heart rate. Miller and DiCara changed the reward to a punishment and this time delivered a mild electrical shock to the tail. The rats learned just as well.

A second line of investigation wanted to show that the new behavior of the paralyzed rats displayed other phenomena associated with the instrumental learning of the somatic nervous system. Every phenomenon that Miller and DiCara looked at, including the ability to "discriminate" and produce new behavior in response to a range of changing stimuli and the ability to retain a newly acquired skill without reinforcement (in Pavlovian conditioning, new behavior becomes "extinct" unless it is reinforced), "turned out to be characteristic of visceral as well as skeletal response."

A third line of investigation explored the still-unsettled issue that, in some subtle way, the rats had acquired their new behavior through the response of their somatic and not their autonomic nervous systems. For example, a case could be made, Miller relentlessly insisted, that the change in heart rates came about from an unobserved skeletal response. Miller and DiCara proceeded to train a variety of visceral responses—stomach contractions, the formation of urine, and blood flow. One visceral response might reasonably be attributed to an unobserved skeletal activity. But could a second, a third, a fourth?

Their success must have been heady. In trying to train blood flow, they set themselves the challenge of having the rats increase the blood in a designated ear. "We were somewhat surprised and greatly delighted," Miller comments, "to find that this experiment actually worked." How much greater specificity could a critic want?

In a long review of all these experiments, Miller acknowledged that a series of questions still awaited answers. Although noncurarized rats could be trained to increase or decrease their heart rates, why was the degree of change they achieved so much smaller than the degree produced by curarized rats? Miller surmised that the curare reduced the "noise" of the physiological system, allowing the rats to concentrate more intently. Later events would force Miller to return to this issue and to reconsider his speculation.

Rats could control their visceral responses, but could humans? The evidence that they could, attained by "the able investigators who have courageously challenged the strong traditional belief in the inferiority of the autonomic nervous system," was mounting. "I believe that in this respect," Miller declared, humans "are as smart as rats."

What about the relation of visceral responses to matters of health? Could visceral learning be a source of psychosomatic symptoms, including cardiovascular disorders and gastric distress? Miller and DiCara were beginning to investigate these issues. Could patients with visceral disorders or any other symptom "under neural control"—cardiac arrhythmias, hypertension, spastic colitis—be trained to "reeducate" their responses? Miller was hopeful, but cautious: "While it is far too early to promise any cures," he concluded his review, "it certainly will be worthwhile to investigate thoroughly the therapeutic possibilities of improved instrumental training techniques."

Whatever the questions, the responses central to the functions of the body were now in hailing distance of the learning mind.

The Advent of Biofeedback

Miller's success in training the responses of the autonomic nervous system, accompanied by the care with which he built his case and considered alternative antagonistic interpretations, and the sheer variety of the responses he trained (salivation, heart rate, intestinal contractions, urinary control, blood flow, and others), was to a dispersed and assorted collection of researchers the equivalent of the electrical stimulation that Miller sent into the brains of rats to reward them.

Many researchers had been exploring ways in which people could learn to gain control of different processes of their bodies (including their brains) for various purposes, from being able to modify physiological reactions to tension and anxiety, to altering physiological processes that contribute to specific physical disorders, to inducing states of consciousness that apparently accompany periods of creativity. The researchers came from a jumble of fields and addressed a jumble of problems. Some studied brain waves, some were concerned with hypnosis, some were developing clinical treatments for particular disorders (from cardiovascular problems to epilepsy), and some studied the control that animals could exert over the physiological and electrical activities of their bodies.

Miller's success became a kind of general validation for all this work and served to bring together the scattered investigators of self-control under the loose heading of biofeedback. The term had been used for several years, but now it was invested with new meaning. It pointed to the possibility of a new kind of medicine, a medicine, as one sober commentator put it, "in which the patient can, for the first time, take a fully active and direct role in literally learning not to be sick."

It did not work out that way. As biofeedback developed specific applications over the years, its focus became narrower and more mechanical, and today it essentially is a congerie of techniques by which one may achieve a degree of control over a limited number of visceral responses. Instead of taking "a fully active and direct role in literally learning not to be sick," a person is attached to a machine that records one or another aspect of the person's visceral behavior, and in response to the absence of a signal indicating that the behavior has passed an acceptable boundary, the person tries to bring the behavior within an appropriate range. What's more, no one knows how this is done, when it is done—not everyone is successful with biofeedback. Presumably it happens the same way that Miller and DiCara's rats learned to raise or lower their heart rates, hardly a basis for learning how not to be sick.

But in the early days of biofeedback—when books on the subject for the public promised miracles around the corner—hopes were high. In 1971, a few years after the studies on visceral learning became known, a publisher of books on behavioral medicine began issuing an annual reader of studies and papers on biofeedback. The series, which lasted eight years, was called *Biofeedback and Self-Control* (Miller was one of its six editors, as was DiCara, until his death in 1976), and no one looking at the first several volumes of the series can miss the underlying feeling of excitement, the sense that the understanding of mind and body might be approaching a revolutionary new stage in medicine.

Interest in biofeedback was so strong that Miller's work on visceral learning brought him a brief spurt of public fame. In 1972, *The New Yorker* published a two-part profile on him (written by Gerald Jonas), and thought that he was enough of a celebrity to announce the profile with a full-page advertisement in *The New York Times.*

An Inexplicable Setback

Miller, for his part, was in his laboratories, and what happened next is one of the most bizarre and inexplicable episodes of contemporary experimental psychology. He found that neither he nor anyone else could replicate his studies on visceral learning.

The problem started when Miller, with a new associate, Barry Dworkin, began to work on new studies and found it difficult to train the heart rates of curarized rats. To satisfy themselves that nothing was wrong with their experimental procedures, which essentially had been handled by DiCara or by Miller's other associates, Dworkin repeated the study in which Miller and DiCara used the reward of electrical stimulation to train curarized rats to raise or lower their heart rates. To Miller and Dworkin's surprise and puzzlement, the experiment, despite repeated efforts, did not work. The rats could not be trained. For one thing, when curarized, their heart rates were extremely high and remarkably unvaried. There often was not enough variation up or down to reward or punish.

Trying to puzzle out what was wrong, Dworkin reviewed all the previous experiments in which curarized rats had been trained to change their heart rates. From 1966 to 1970, there were eight such studies in Miller's laboratory and two studies in other laboratories. When Dworkin had the intuition to arrange the studies chronologically, he and Miller discovered, to their consternation, that the achieved changes had become progressively smaller. In the first studies, Miller and DiCara had trained their rats to decrease or increase their heart rates by an average of 15 to 20 percent. In the last studies, the percentage had dwindled to an average of 5 to 10 percent. The decline in between had been steady. The results were now "hovering near the zero mark."

Miller has written that he was "greatly puzzled and disappointed," but he approached the problem as if he himself had nothing at stake. Throughout this remarkable episode, he acted with the fearlessness of a person interested only in the truth.

"We thought in learning what was wrong and how to correct it we might discover something that would help us to improve human visceral learning and perhaps would even have therapeutic value. Our difficulties could turn out to be a disguised opportunity if we only had the wit to comprehend what they were telling us."

While Miller and Dworkin conducted their own intense study of the problem, Miller began talking about it at scientific meetings. He described the nature of the problem, the failed explanations they had tried so far, and the areas of inquiry they were still exploring. He asked his colleagues for help. Did they know of similar experiences? Did they have any suggestions that might explain what had happened?

Miller had the idea that the problem might be the rats. Maybe they were being bred differently. Miller learned that rats were now fed a better diet, were handled less, and were shipped to suppliers by air express rather than rail. All these changes, along with others, reduced the stress the rats encountered before ending up in a laboratory. Perhaps the changes eliminated the "kinds of stresses that could be necessary for the development of capacities for visceral learning."

Miller obtained rats from other than his usual suppliers, but it made no difference. The rats might have been the problem, but nothing that Miller found out or tried could help him decide one way or the other.

Maybe the curare was the problem. After one of Miller's public presentations of his frustrating difficulties, he learned that curare was an imperfectly purified drug and that it could vary from year to year "much as wine varies from vintage to vintage." This lead was another dead end.

Maybe the problem had nothing to do with the experiments. Miller remembered that when he began the experiments, the room that held the animal subjects had been sprayed to rid it of a bedbug infestation. Maybe the residue of the spray had been responsible for the ability of the rats to train their visceral responses. Dworkin injected minute amounts of the chemical spray into the rats he and Miller were now working with. It made no difference. "I have not yet had the courage," Miller told an audience, "to suggest introducing an epidemic of bedbugs."

Perhaps the experiments were not what they seemed. Perhaps the results were an artifact of an unnoticed feature of the experiments. "In my present state of intense perplexity and vexation, having lost many hours of sleep puzzling about the problem," Miller once declared, "I would welcome anything, even a plausible artifact, that would reproduce the original effects." Miller assigned "a naturally skeptical and ingenious postdoctoral student" to the problem. But nothing the researcher did produced the original results.

Miller even considered the possibility that he and his colleagues had suffered from a form of mass hallucination. The evidence made it unlikely. Many people were involved, both participants and observers, and some details of the experiments remained so vivid, he could not believe that he had imagined them. He remembered an uncomfortable experience standing with DiCara, watching a rat who could turn off the electric shock to the tail only by lowering its heart rate. The rat instead had increased its heart rate, and the rate seemingly would not go down. The rat continued to receive the electric shock. "We stood until we could not bear watching any longer and then walked out of the room to get a Coke, returning to find that the rat had finally come down to meet the criterion and now was proceeding to learn the demanded increases." Could such an episode be part of a mass hallucination?

For five years, Miller and Dworkin tried to find the answer. In 1977, they acknowledged defeat. Neither they nor anyone else could replicate the experiments or understand why they could not. For Miller and anyone else concerned with visceral learning, it was time to move on, to pursue the question in other ways. Miller wrote: "It is prudent not to rely on any of the experiments on curarized animals for evidence on the instrumental learning of visceral responses."

Moving on to Human Subjects

Miller was pleased to note that there was human evidence for investigators of visceral learning to consider. He took pixie-ish delight in talking about the control of the urinary sphinters. The urinary sphincters are known to be under the control of the autonomic nervous system, which means, in the traditional view, that they cannot be trained and controlled. But of course they are (most of the time). He told one of his audiences, "I trust that all of you have learned to control urination under the favorable conditions of strong motivation and immediate knowledge of results."

Miller's listeners would have had an easy reply: Like many activities that are under the domain of the autonomic nervous system, the urinary sphincters can also be activated or controlled by the somatic nervous system. The capacity of the somatic nervous system to influence visceral responses is the reason, of course, that Miller had paralyzed his rats: to make sure that the somatic nervous system was not doing the work of the autonomic responses that he was attempting to train. Many autonomic responses can be activated by somatic interventions. "A crude example," Miller once explained, "is putting a finger down the throat to induce vomiting." As for urination, it can be induced by using the abdominal muscles to increase pressure on the bladder "until stimulation of stretch receptors elicits reflex emptying."

Miller thought that visceral learning could also be involved in the control of the urinary sphincters. He pointed to a little-known study conducted in the mid-1950s, a few years before he began his own work on visceral learning. Researchers had paralyzed 16 people, some with curare, some with another paralytic drug, succinylcholine. The subjects thus lost control of their somatic nervous systems and all the skeletal responses that they commanded. (Like Miller's rats, the subjects also had to be maintained on artificial respiration.) Now, if control of the urinary sphincters depended only on skeletal responses, then in a paralyzed state, the control would be lost. Yet the paralyzed subjects "could initiate urination on command about as fast as ever and could stop it in about twice the time required before paralysis." Even though "all effects of overt contraction of the skeletal musculature were ruled out," the subjects could still exercise a "learned voluntary control" over urination—which meant that the "learned voluntary control" in this case had taken place in the autonomic nervous system.

In the early 1970s, as Miller was striving to understand why it no longer seemed possible to train curarized rats, he and some of his students began working with hospitalized patients who, through illnesses or accidents, had lost control of various somatically controlled processes and systems of their bodies. If Miller could teach such patients to regain some of their lost control, the change would have to have occurred through the still-operative autonomic nervous system. Whether he could be successful was unclear. He had never been able to achieve large changes in rats that were not curarized, and he had not applied his techniques to human beings with severe disabilities.

Miller began by trying to lower the high blood pressure of patients with polio or muscular dystrophy. He was only minimally successful. He was not sure why. The patients were able to lower their blood pressure somewhat, but not enough to matter.

In the hospital in which Miller was working, a 31-year-old man whose spinal cord had been severed by a gunshot several years earlier heard about the people who were trying to train patients to control their blood pressure. The man had an unusual and particularly severe blood pressure problem. Most people have blood pressure that is too high. His was too low—that is, once he pulled himself to an upright position on crutches, his blood pressure would quickly drop so low that in a matter of minutes he would faint. The gunshot had interrupted the ordinary autonomic processes by which an adequate level of blood pressure is maintained when a person stands up.

The man and his physical therapists had made strenuous efforts to deal with the problem. One strategy for the man was to move towards an upright position in carefully calculated stages. But none of the strategies worked. The man had struggled to make his arms strong enough to hold him up on crutches, but it appeared that he had been defeated by his low blood pressure.

The man asked a member of the hospital staff who was working with Miller, Bernard Brucker, to help him. Would Brucker teach him how to raise his pressure?

Both Brucker and Miller knew that virtually all efforts to help people control their blood pressure had been directed at people whose pressure was too high. Now here was a man who wanted to learn to raise his abnormally low blood pressure, who had to learn to raise it to a height that was more than twice the level to which it would fall after he stood up, and what was worse, whose usual autonomic process of maintaining an adequate level of blood pressure had been injured. It was almost impossible to see how the man could use other features of the autonomic system to correct the precipitous drop in his pressure. Brucker described the man as "the least likely candidate, from a neurological perspective, to successfully learn voluntary control of blood pressure." But the man persisted, and Brucker finally agreed to try and help him.

The training program consisted of a total of eleven hour-long sessions, one a day, four times a week. A blood pressure cuff was wrapped around one of the man's arms and was connected to a mechanism that set off a tone whenever he produced the appropriate change in his blood pressure. The training was aimed at teaching the man to both raise and lower his pressure. By learning to do both, he presumably would become more adept at each skill separately.

At the start of the training, the man was told to try to raise or lower his blood pressure simply "by concentrating on either increased or decreased blood pressure." The man worked with the machine, with Brucker, and with himself. He would try to raise (or lower) his blood pressure for one to three five-minute trials a session. At the end of each trial,

Brucker would discuss with the man the magnitude and direction of the changes he had produced. Brucker would also ask him if he could feel any of the changes and if he knew what he had done to produce them.

As the training progressed, the man reported that he felt sensations of dizziness when the pressure was low and "a feeling of pressure and pulse beat in his head, accompanied by sweating when his pressure was high." By the end of the sessions, the man could increase and decrease his blood pressure "using his own sensations of pressure change as feedback." He continued to train himself for another four months, and against all the neurological odds, succeeded in learning how to raise his blood pressure high enough that he could walk on crutches.

Miller and Brucker had accomplished what they had no good reason to believe that they could accomplish. Mysteriously, patients with polio or muscular dystrophy had shown little ability to "learn large increases in blood pressure." Yet this man with a severed spinal cord, "the least likely candidate, from a neurological perspective, to successfully learn voluntary control of blood pressure," had managed to do it.

Miller and Brucker began training nine other patients with spinal cord lesions. With one to five training sessions, all the patients succeeded in raising their average blood pressure about a third of the height reached by the first man.

For seven patients, there was nothing to be gained by any further increase and so no compelling reason to continue. (In biofeedback with humans, the rewards and punishments come from the subjects themselves. Because the person wants to control the response—the rats in Miller's experiments had no such desire—the signal that the person has achieved control is the reward, the lack of a signal the punishment. If the person has nothing to gain, there is no reward, and hence no incentive to succeed.) But two patients, one of them paralyzed from the neck down, suffered from blood pressure levels that were even lower than the pressure of the first man Brucker had trained. They would faint in their wheelchairs if their feet were not kept at about the level of their heads. These two patients continued their efforts to increase their blood pressure.

After a substantial number of training sessions—about twice the number conducted with the first man—both patients were able to produce and maintain a high enough pressure to enable them to sit in their wheelchairs with their feet down.

In marshaling the evidence to support the conclusion that the patients' new ability to control blood pressure levels was gained through the training of their autonomic nervous systems, Miller and Brucker faced the old question: How could one be sure that the learning had not been performed by the somatic nervous system? Unlike the rats, the patients could breathe on their own, and since pressure goes up when people quicken their breathing and goes down when breathing is slowed, perhaps the patients had somehow maneuvered their respiratory systems to raise their pressure.

Miller and Brucker carefully tested the breathing patterns and muscular contractions of the patients as they increased their blood pressure. There was no evidence that either process contributed to the increase.

Referring to the man paralyzed from the neck down, the most incapacitated of the patients, and alluding by implication to all the other patients, Miller and Brucker declared that "although it is difficult to rule out completely the possibility that this patient with extremely limited control over skeletal musculature hit upon some subtle skeletal response" to manipulate his blood pressure, the possibility "seems unlikely." In their view, "the evidence on patients with spinal lesions supports the notion that human subjects can instrumentally learn to achieve specific, direct, voluntary control over a visceral response such as blood pressure."

Still, there was a problem. Why were patients with spinal lesions able to produce large changes in blood pressure while other patients immobilized by polio and muscular dystrophy were not? What was the difference? Why couldn't every patient do it?

Miller had considered variations of this question before. He originally had wondered why he could produce large visceral changes in curarized rats but only small ones in noncurarized rats. He had speculated then that the curare cut down on distracting "noise," enabling a rat to concentrate more fully on the task at hand.

When he discovered that his original experiments could not be replicated and that it had become impossible to train the visceral responses of curarized rats, he wondered why the first group of curarized rats had been so responsive and all the rest so unresponsive. He proposed that the answer might have something to do with the self-regulatory process by which an organism always tries to keep itself in a relative state of equilibrium. For example, a person who is cold starts to shiver, a person who is hot starts to perspire. The shivering and the perspiration are attempts to keep the body's temperature within fairly circumscribed limits. The name for this process is homeostasis.

Miller suggested that he had somehow interfered with the homeostatic control in the original curarized rats but that, without understanding the reason, had not interfered with it in the succeeding rats. The same process, he contended, might explain the much greater rate of change in curarized than in noncurarized rats. Maybe the difference had nothing to do with cancelling the "noise" that presumably distracted nonparalyzed rats. Perhaps the explanation was that he again had somehow interfered with the homeostatic controls of the curarized rats. As long as the homeostatic controls are in place, he proposed, the visceral changes would be small: The presence of the controls would prevent any large changes in the responses of the autonomic nervous system.

He and Brucker now suggested that the same general consideration might explain the apparently special capacity of people with spinal lesions to control their blood pressure. Perhaps, like the curare in the first set of experiments, the lesions somehow interfered with the homeostatic mechanisms, thereby freeing the patients, as the curare may have freed the rats, to exercise a substantial control over their visceral responses.

Might it be possible to learn how to interfere with the homeostatic mechanism at will, Miller wondered, and allow people the full opportunity, when they needed it, to train the responses of their trainable autonomic nervous systems? The question, which remains unexplored, points to the current limits of biofeedback.

The Status of Biofeedback Today

Biofeedback techniques, like relaxation methods, are applied to a variety of disorders and, despite the basic difference between relaxation and biofeedback—relaxation aims for a general calming of many physiological processes, biofeedback aims for the control of an individual response, which it seeks to increase or decrease—both are useful for many of the same disorders, including headaches, pain, hypertension, and insomnia. Biofeedback is also used in treating neurological motor problems and gastrointestinal problems. It is the only treatment for fecal incontinence.

As with relaxation, there is no doubt that biofeedback helps many people and brings relief for many physical disorders. Medicine would be poorer without it. Yet it essentially remains an alternative treatment, or a treatment used in support of other treatments. Often the relief it offers is statistically no more than the relief provided by one or another relaxation method. For disorders that can be treated with drugs as well as biofeedback, the drugs usually offer greater relief. Biofeedback has brought the mind into the body in a more decisive way than relaxation has—the mind in biofeedback tries to move directly into the body to teach its physiology new behavior—but biofeedback has not been able to penetrate very far.

The question that hangs over biofeedback is the question that Miller addressed in his speculations about a homeostatic mechanism. Miller's powerful work on visceral learning produced changes that were deep and extensive, that had the promise of being limitless. Biofeedback swept in on this promise and the hope that human beings might soon be able to apply their minds in a systematic way to moderate or correct a large variety of the body's most nagging and recalcitrant ills and even some of its major diseases. Today, the changes effected by biofeedback are small, occur in a scattered collection of disorders, and are not certain. Some people can achieve them, some cannot. A piece is missing, but where or what it is remains unclear.

Miller's great achievement was to wrest the autonomic nervous system from the brute world of mechanical physiology and give it its proper place, in the body that has a mind—even if, to Miller, the mind is a brain. It seems only a stroke of bad luck that he has not been able to uncover more fully the place where mind and body meet.

The Biofeedback "Mind"

The "mind" of biofeedback and of visceral learning is distinct from the "mind" of Type A (and hostility) and the "mind" of the relaxation response, and is one more "mind" to add to the list of "minds" that can move the body. In Type A, the "mind" is the "mind" of emotion; in the relaxation response it is the "mind" that snaps itself into an act of concentration that has no content; in biofeedback, it is the "mind" of trial-and-error learning. We all know this "mind." It is the tool we use to master many of our skills, including the skills we use to move our bodies through the world. Miller has shown that we can use it to move some of the internal elements of our bodies too.

These "minds" may be connected. Miller would probably say that the "emotional mind" is an offshoot of the "trial-and-error mind": We may learn our emotions as responses to the stimuli of our experiences. But in different mind-body studies, each of these "minds" is an independent and self-sufficient entity, and each is capable of altering processes of the body.

Yet in the sense that none of these "minds" acts on the body directly and deliberately, they are closely alike. The "emotional mind" has no idea that it is inducing the physiological changes that later may lead to discomfort or illness. The "snap-on mind" of the relaxation response knows it wants to achieve a certain sense of calm, but it does not know how to address the body directly and ask for the calm. It must shift itself into low gear through an act of concentration and then let this low gear do the work the "mind" cannot do for itself.

With the "trial-and-error mind," the "mind" does its job through a form of chance. It knows where it wants to go, but it does not know how to get there. It stumbles forward in trial-and-error movement until, in time and with luck, it finds the right path, or a part of it. For animals the picture is a bit more complicated. It may take a while for a rat being shocked through its tail to realize that the shock has something to do with its heart rate. But once the rat understands it (in whatever way rats understand), the "mind" it calls upon is no different from the "mind" that a human subject of biofeedback calls upon. This is the "mind" that has no plan, that proceeds in fits and starts, and that does not know how it arrived at its goal after it gets there. This is the "mind" that often must depend on outside authorities—

usually a piece of mechanical equipment—to learn if it has been successful.

When this "mind" tries to speak to the body, it mumbles and does not complete sentences, and hopes to hear back that it has been understood.

CHAPTER 4

Robert Ader,
the Sophisticated Immune System,
and Psychoneuroimmunology

When a few of his rats died on the 45th day of a taste-aversion experiment, Robert Ader, an experimental psychologist whose primary interest was the psychosomatic character of disease, was puzzled. Using a variation of classical Pavlovian conditioning, he had conditioned the rats to have an aversion to the taste of saccharin and was observing them to see how long the aversion lasted. He had conducted such experiments before, and none of the animal subjects had ever died. He could not understand why any were dying now. More died over the next few days.

Still, the deaths had no practical effect on the experiment. In about a week's time, Ader determined that the taste aversion had lasted 50 days. Effects elicited with Pavlovian conditioning gradually wear off if they are not reinforced. When Ader learned that it took 50 days for the taste aversion to be extinguished, he had learned what he needed to know, and he concluded the experiment. He would write later that he had concluded it "prematurely"—he had not understood what he had observed.

Ader is a man who does not like loose ends, and the deaths

continued to puzzle him. He wondered if they could have anything to do with the chemical he had used to create the taste aversion. Ader had injected the rats with a substance called cyclophosphamide, which causes rats to experience the equivalent of nausea. Immediately afterward, he gave the rats a saccharin-flavored drink. He wanted the rats to associate the flavor with the effects of the cyclophosphamide and, as a result, develop an aversion to the flavor. Ader found that the aversion developed after only one pairing of drink and chemical. He determined how long the aversion lasted by continuing to give the rats the saccharin-flavored liquid and seeing how much of it they would drink. After 50 days, they treated it as if it was no different from water. The aversion had worn off. And, mysteriously, a number of rats had died.

Ader had had no particular reason to use cyclophosphamide. He could just as well have used a chemical called lithium which also causes stomach upset in rats. When he researched the properties of cyclophosphamide, Ader discovered that in addition to eliciting nausea, it also suppressed certain reactions of the immune system. The immune system is regarded as the body's primary line of defense against the entities of the environment that can enter the body and promote illness. When an immune system is weakened, it cannot provide its usual degree of defense and an organism has an increased chance of getting sick.

The breathtaking idea struck Ader that in more or less randomly picking cyclophosphamide to elicit an aversion to saccharin, he had inadvertently created a situation in which the rats had also been conditioned to weaken their own immune systems. The rats, he reasoned, had come to invest saccharin with both the nausea-causing and immune-suppressing effects of cyclophosphamide, so every time the rats took a drink of saccharin and "thought" it was cyclophosphamide (as Pavlov's dog "thought" the bell was food), both effects followed—the nausea and the immune suppression.

From his data, Ader learned that the rats that died were the ones that had drunk the most saccharin-flavored liquid. It seemed to him that he had taught them to do by themselves what the drug would do. If he was right, the events of the experiment had shown that the immune system could be influenced by what an organism believed—by what went on in the brain.

This idea—and the remarkable possibility that it might be demonstrated in a laboratory—ran directly counter to the established understanding of the immune system, an understanding that had grown ever since the immune system had been discovered in the last decades of the 19th century by a man who stuck a thorn in a starfish and watched a growing number of cells move to engulf the thorn. The immune system was of the body, it protected the body, but it gave itself its own orders. The evidence was clear. One could take a drop of blood from the body and put the blood on a slide and introduce a pathogen into it, and the immune cells in the blood would respond to the pathogen, without any directions from a brain or anything else. The immune system needed no help in knowing what to do and then doing it. It was independent and sovereign. For all the years that it had been studied, almost no one other than a number of psychologists had seen the need to introduce the possibility that the immune system might have anything to do with the mind.

Like the autonomic nervous system before Neal Miller forced a reexamination of it, the immune system was held to be fundamentally self-regulating and autonomous. The critical difference between the systems was that the autonomic nervous system had been viewed as dumb and the immune system was viewed as sophisticated, perhaps the smartest system within the body. Neal Miller's colleagues may have considered him slightly mad for believing that one could train the responses of the autonomic nervous system, but at least the system was primitive and Miller had studied and worked with its responses—he had earned the right to have a bizarre idea. But if immunologists were to hear that a *psy-*

chologist thought that the immune system might be susceptible to the influence of the brain, they most likely would consider such a person unknowledgeable at best and a fool at
worst. One did not understand the immune system overnight.

The implications of demonstrating that the immune system was in contact with the brain were so large that Ader
took the unusual step of sending a "communication" to a
research journal, *Psychosomatic Medicine,* to explain the opportunity he now had—to investigate the "intriguing possibility" of eliciting a "behaviorally conditioned immunosuppres-
sion." (Ader at this point, sticking to the facts as he knew
them, spoke only of suppressing the immune system and not
more generally of altering it, either up or down.) If this could
be done, if one could condition an organism to suppress the
responses of its immune system, it would raise "innumerable
issues concerning the normal operation and modifiability of
the immune system." Could immune response be influenced
by mental phenomena other than conditioning techniques?
Could mental events be involved in the "normal operation"
of the immune system?

The conditioning of immune responses would also suggest
the possibility of "a mechanism that may be involved in the
complex pathogenesis of psychosomatic disease." If immune
responses could be influenced by mental events, it was conceivable (as Neal Miller argued with regard to visceral responses) that such events could be a factor in the development of disease. All of these issues, Ader implied, might now
be susceptible to controlled experimental analysis.

The "potential significance" of conditioning immune responses, Ader wrote in the flat language of science, "seemed
to justify this preliminary communication in an effort to
stimulate the broadest possible approach to an analysis of
this phenomenon."

Early Psychosomatic Studies of Gastric Ulcers

From the start of his career in the late 1950s, Ader has been concerned with the mix of physiological and psychological circumstances that together can establish the conditions for disease. For Ader, disease—illness in general—does not come from a single physiological or psychological "cause." Disease is psychosomatic. It arises from a constellation of elements and circumstances, physiological and psychological. No one element is central; no one element is more important than another. Disease comes from the combination and interrelationship of all the elements.

In the 1960s, Ader conducted a model series of experiments exploring the effect of different combinations of psychological and physiological elements on the development of gastric ulcers in rats. He chose gastric ulcers because "ulcers in man is probably *the* classic example of a 'psychosomatic disease.'" (His quotation marks mean that he does not accept the standard notion that some diseases are psychosomatic and some are not.) He chose rats because one can produce gastric ulcers in rats simply by restraining them for a number of hours. In simple and general terms, the restraint leads to a "feeling," the feeling leads to the release of certain secretions from the gastric glands, the secretions lead to ulcers. Given this established sequence of events, Ader could examine how physiological or psychological factors, singly or together, might hasten, retard, or otherwise modify the development of ulcers.

In one of his first experiments, he explored the findings of studies by other researchers that a high level of pepsinogen, a chemical secreted by the gastric glands, is statistically associated with ulcers. Ader took two groups of rats, one with high levels of pepsinogen and one with low levels, and restrained both of them the same amount of time—long enough for gastric lesions to appear. Put another way, to two contrasting levels of pepsinogen, he added the same amount of "stress." (Ader argues that there no such entity as "stress." The word obscures the very mixture of events and circumstances that he wants to clarify. Ader is not the only person to disapprove of the concept of stress, but he may be the most rigorous.)

On the face of it, Ader's findings are no surprise: A larger percentage of rats with high levels of pepsinogen (6 out of 21) developed gastric lesions than did rats with low levels of pepsinogen (1 out of 25). But for Ader, the findings had a more complex meaning. Since 15 of the rats with high levels of pepsinogen did not develop lesions, it was clear that high levels of pepsinogen plus a component of "stress" did not always lead to ulcers. Either another contributing factor was necessary or a mitigating factor had weakened the combined effect of pepsinogen and "stress." Further, since one of the rats with low levels of pepsinogen did develop a lesion, it was also clear that even a rat with a low level of pepsinogen could develop an ulcer in the presence of other factors (one of which was probably the "stress" of restraint).

In succeeding experiments, Ader explored some of the other factors and their interrelationships. In one study, Ader considered the possible impact of the psychological element of "attitudes" or "perceptions." He reasoned that an animal that was more psychologically troubled by an event—by restraint, for example—would be more likely to develop stomach lesions than would a less troubled animal. But how could one know if a rat was more or less troubled? What was the equivalent in a rat of an attitude or perception?

Rats, it turns out, have cyclic patterns of activity. At one point in the cycle, they are very active; at another point, they are relatively quiescent. Ader speculated that rats that were restrained during the period of high activity would be "more troubled" by the restraint than would rats that were restrained during the quiescent period of the cycle.

Ader again had a group of rats with high levels of pepsinogen and another group with low levels, and again he restrained both groups. But he now introduced a variation in choosing when to apply the restraint. In each group, he restrained half of the rats during the period of high activity and half during the period of low activity. He found that the rats that were restrained at the peaks of their activity cycles—and so presumably felt more frustrated by the restraint—were significantly more likely to develop gastric erosions. This was true whether the rats had high or low levels of pepsinogen. The factor of "attitude" (when the restraint was applied) made the impact of the factor of "stress" (the restraint) more or less serious.

From Ader's perspective, the study supported the idea that no factor has an intrinsic effect in and of itself in the development of disease (many mind-body studies assume otherwise), but is always modulated by the presence or absence of other factors.

In one of Ader's most intriguing experiments, he subtly examined the combined effects of a psychological factor from the past and a psychological factor from the present. Studies had shown that rats that had been subjected to discomfort during their three-week period of preweaning were more likely to develop a disease than rats that had been treated well during this period. Other studies had shown that rats that lived alone were less likely to contract a disease than rats that lived in groups. In Ader's study, preweaning treatment represented the psychological factor of the past, housing conditions represented the psychological factor of the present.

Ader this time used three groups of rats. One group was stroked or petted daily during the three weeks of preweaning, a second group received a daily electric shock during the same period, the third group, the controls, was neither stroked nor shocked. After the preweaning period, Ader sub-

77

divided each group. One subgroup lived alone, the other lived in clusters of five or six rats. Ader then subjected all the rats to 18 hours of immobilization.

One finding might have been expected. The rats that had been stroked during their infancy were least susceptible to developing gastric lesions, the rats that had been shocked were most susceptible. The controls, neither stroked nor shocked, were in between. So far, so good: A "pleasant" childhood reduced the likelihood of gastric lesions; a "nasty" childhood increased the likelihood.

But the picture was importantly modified by the ways in which the past and present affected each other. When the rats that had been shocked during preweaning lived in groups, all of them—100 percent—developed ulcers. But when they lived alone, only 80 percent developed ulcers, the same percentage of control rats to develop ulcers. In other words, when they lived alone, their rate of disease was no different from the rate among rats that had had a more or less "ordinary" rat childhood. It seemed that a "good" present wiped away the effect of a "bad" past.

As Ader put it, "the effects of intervention during the course of development [receiving daily shocks during preweaning] are capable of being modified by subsequent social or environmental influences."

On the other hand, the past could affect the present. While a "good" present might wipe away a "bad" past, the effects of a "bad" present were influenced by whether the past was "good" or "bad." The shocked rats that lived in groups did worse than the stroked rats that lived in groups. "Environmental stimulation, in this instance, differential housing, elicits psychophysiological changes . . . that are determined in part by the psychophysiological background upon which that form of environmental stimulation is superimposed." The past was not etched in stone, but it could make a difference.

In the late 1960s and early 1970s, Ader published several papers in which he attempted to organize in schematic fash-

78

ion the psychosomatic assortment of factors that can increase an organism's susceptibility to disease. But then his rats died, and he was presented with an extraordinary opportunity to explore a psychosomatic phenomenon of major proportions: the possibility that the immune system was not an inviolable, self-regulating, autonomous unit within the body but a system that sometimes took its cues from the dictates of the mind—or, in Ader's language, the central nervous system, the system through which an organism receives information from the environment and responds to the information, both outwardly and in the functioning body.

The Conditioning Experiments

Ader's first conditioning experiment took nine days. He worked with immunologist Nicholas Cohen, who has remained Ader's partner in their continuing investigations of an immune system that can receive signals from outside itself. Ader and Cohen basically repeated the events that Ader inadvertently initiated in his study of taste aversion, but this time in a controlled situation.

On the first day of the experiment, Ader and Cohen set up three groups of rats. The researchers gave one group an injection of cyclophosphamide and paired it with a drink of saccharin-flavored liquid in such a way that the rats associated the drink with the effects of the drug. This was the conditioned group. If Ader and Cohen were right—if the rats had been conditioned to respond to the liquid as if it were the drug—then once the rats had another drink of the liquid, the result would be a weakened immune reaction.

Ader and Cohen gave a second group of rats the drug and the drink, but this time in such a way that the rats would not associate them. This was the nonconditioned group. According to Ader and Cohen's expectations, further drinks of the

saccharine-flavored liquid would have no effect on the immune reactions of these rats.

With the third group, Ader and Cohen gave an injection of a neutral substance that had no effect on the immune system and the usual saccharin-flavored drink. This was the control group. It had received nothing to suppress the immune system, and it represented the normal level of response in the immune system of rats.

On the second day of the experiment, the rats drank only tap water.

On the third day of the experiment, Ader and Cohen injected all the rats with a foreign material that is commonly used to test immune reactions (red blood cells of sheep). Thirty minutes later, Ader and Cohen gave the conditioned and nonconditioned rats their second drink of the saccharin-flavored liquid. If Ader and Cohen were right, the response of the conditioned rats to the drink should lead to a weakened immune reaction against the foreign material. In the nonconditioned rats, the liquid should have no effect on the immune reactions.

On the ninth day of the study, Ader and Cohen drew blood samples from all the rats to measure their immune reactions. The two men might have scripted the results. The conditioned rats had the lowest immune reaction, the control rats (which had had no suppressants) the highest, and the nonconditioned rats (which had had an injection of the immune-suppressing drug on the first day) a reaction level somewhere in between.

Both the conditioned and nonconditioned rats had all received an injection of the drug, and both had all received two drinks of the saccharin-flavored liquid. Yet the immune reactions of the conditioned rats were significantly lower than the immune reactions of the nonconditioned rats. In the terms of the study, there was only one factor that could explain such a difference: Conditioning had led the rats to suppress their own immune reactions. This was the point that Ader

80

and Cohen were aiming for. The rats had "told" their immune systems what to do, and the immune system had responded.

Ader and Cohen performed a number of experiments to make sure that the results could not be attributed somehow to another factor, the drug, for example, or even the saccharin-flavored liquid. They did the experiment with a different immune-suppressing drug (methotrexate). They did it with a differently flavored liquid (sucrose). The results were the same.

In one study they tested the possibility that the suppression of the immune reaction might be caused by thirst. Perhaps the conditioned rats, which in the course of being conditioned had developed a taste aversion, were not drinking enough. Ader and Cohen demonstrated that even when conditioned rats were sated with water, they still wound up with a suppressed immune reaction.

The two researchers turned to another consideration. All the experiments so far had involved the suppression of an immune reaction that consisted of releasing chemical substances called antibodies. But the immune system also sometimes releases cells to deal with foreign invaders. (The releease of antibodies is a called a humoral response, the release of cells simply a cellular response.) Could rats also suppress a cellular response of the immune system?

Ader and Cohen (sometimes working with another colleague, Dana Bovbjerg) performed the experiment with a substance (foreign lymphocytes) that provoked a cellular immune response. The results were the same. The conditioned rates showed the lowest response, the control rats the highest, and the nonconditioned rats, which had received a dose of an immune-suppressing drug, a response that was in between.

Other laboratories had already begun to confirm Ader and Cohen's basic finding, and a laboratory in Canada, headed by Reginald Gorcynski, supplied an important extension. All of Ader and Cohen's experiments and the experiments that replicated their work dealt with immune suppression. Gorcynski and his colleagues showed that it was also possible to use conditioning to bring about an enhanced immune reaction.

Gorcynski grafted onto one species of mice the skin from another species and then wrapped bandages around the grafts. Because the grafts came from a different species, they were foreign material, and in such a case (in graft situations in general), the host responds with an outpouring of immune cells to destroy the invader. In other words, there is an enhanced immune reaction.

Gorcynski removed the grafts and the bandages after 9 days. During this time, the host mice had shown an elevated immune reaction. In the next 40 days, Gorcynski repeated the grafts-and-bandages procedure on the same mice another two times. Each time the mice showed an elevated immune reaction.

Through this repetition of grafts and bandages, Gorcynski had conditioned the mice to associate the bandages with the grafts. Gorcynski now faked a graft on the mice. He applied bandages just as if they were a wrapping around a graft, but there was no graft. Yet for the mice, the bandages had "become" the grafts, and the mice reacted as they had before, with an elevated immune reaction. In all the previous procedures, the grafts had provoked the reaction. This time, the mice did it.

Just as Ader and Cohen had created a situation in which rats were led to suppress an immune reaction, Gorcynski and his colleagues had created a situation in which mice were led to enhance an immune reaction.

Gorcynski's study completed a circle. The control of the mind (the brain, the central nervous system) over the immune system was not limited to changes in one direction. The control extended in both directions. Depending on the message, an immune reaction could be suppressed or enhanced.

The Naming of Psychoneuroimmunology

At the time that he was conducting his studies on the conditioning of immune reactions, Ader knew that a variety of other kinds of studies were also exploring the possible connections between the central nervous system and the immune system. Some studies wanted to associate the appearance or development of immune-related disease with "stressful" life experiences. Other studies looked at the effects of "stress" just on immune activity. Still other studies had begun to identify physiological mechanisms that in a literal, physical sense could connect the central nervous system to the immune system. If the brain could influence immune activity, there had to be a physiological pathway or network to do it.

He soon became aware of work he had not known about. He learned that about a decade before he began his conditioning studies, another American, George Solomon, an adventurous and original researcher, had for a while teamed up variously with a psychologist (Rudolf Moos) and an immunologist (Alfred Amkraut) to study the connections among emotions, immunity, and disease, and that Solomon had coined the term "psychoimmunology" to describe the phenomenon he believed he had identified.

Ader also learned that there existed a block of Russian studies on conditioning immune responses and that the studies included a vigorous controversy over what conditioning could or could not do. Ader had many of the relevant articles translated so that he could study them.

It was clear to Ader that this assorted and scattered work and his own studies on conditioning were all facets of a single rich investigation. Ader had started his conditioning studies in 1974. A few years later, he began editing a book that would bring all this material together. Ader commissioned overview surveys of all the major research exploring the connections between the central nervous and immune systems, including the connection extending back from the immune system to the central nervous system. (Certain physiological studies had shown that the chemical traffic between the two systems moved both ways.)

The book he called *Psychoneuroimmunology* appeared in 1981. With this title—by which Ader means to trace a line from the psyche through the nervous system to the immune system—and the collection, Ader created what is quickly becoming a new field of study. He showed that the phenomenon that he was documenting in rigorous laboratory investigations and that appeared in his work as an example of conditioning was also at the center of many other kinds of studies that sought to examine the connection between the mind and the body. He brought into one arena many seemingly different lines of research, and without any effort to weave them together, by simply juxtaposing them, he illuminated the features that made them part of a common endeavor.

Psychoneuroimmunology begins with the investigations that most visibly reveal the capacity of the central nervous system to affect the immune system, and through it the health of the body—studies of the association between stressful experiences and immune-related diseases. It concludes with the highly technical investigations of the complex physiological events by which the central nervous system and the immune system communicate with each other. Another way of describing the book's contents and organization is to say that it moves from questions that nearly everyone cares about—such as what makes people sick—to questions that specialists primarily care about: What happens deep in the body when the central nervous system sends messages to the immune system? In between these endpoints the book includes Ader's review of the Russian studies on the conditioning of immune responses, Ader and Cohen's discussion of their own conditioning work and related studies, articles by George Solomon (the man who antedated Ader's "psychoneuroimmunology" by 10 years with his own "psychoimmunology") on the relation of personality to rheumatoid arthritis and the immunological abnormalities that appear in people who are mentally ill, and discussions of the effects of stress on the immune responses of both animals and human beings.

The book provides no definitive answers to any of the large questions that it implicitly poses. But in its elaboration of data of many sorts, *Psychoneuroimmunology* shows that there is strong and varied evidence that the immune system, far from being locked pristinely within itself, is as open as a sieve to the impacts of experience and to the highly elaborate chemical entities that cascade down and out from the central nervous system.

The concept of psychoneuroimmunology has not quite brought Ader public fame, but the word has edged its way into the higher levels of public awareness. It has also gained a certain vogue among researchers looking for an umbrella concept to explain the effects of the mind on the body. But as Ader would be the first to say, psychoneuroimmunology is about specific systems of the body—the immune system in particular—not about the body as a whole, and as a term it explains nothing: It says only that the psyche can influence the activities of the immune system. How extensive that influence can be, and how it may combine with other physiological and psychological elements, is still to be examined.

In 1987, continuing and extending his work as archivist, orchestrator, and, to an extent, arbiter of the field of psychoneuroimmunology, Ader became the editor-in-chief of a new journal, *Brain, Behavior, and Immunity,* "a euphonious euphemism for all aspects of the interactions among behavioral, neuroanatomical, neuroendocrine, neurochemical, and immune processes," a description that evokes Ader's broad psychosomatic approach to bodily phenomena.

The Placebo Offshoot

A funny thing happened in the process by which Ader and Cohen conditioned a rat so that it would respond to a saccharin-flavored liquid by suppressing its own immune system: They created a placebo. A placebo is a substance or an event that has no intrinsic capacity to change the health of an organism, yet, for some organisms, on some occasions, it does. A saccharin-flavored liquid has no intrinsic capacity to suppress the immune activity of a rat that drinks it, yet for the rats that Ader and Cohen conditioned, it had that effect. More correctly, it jogged something in the rat's brain, or wherever else it may store the recollection of its experiences, and this jog set off an uncertain number of events at the end of which the rat had suppressed its immune system.

All placebos begin in the head (the mind, the brain, the central nervous system). The thing that is the placebo cannot by itself bring about any physiological changes. The changes occur only because the organism "believes" they should be happening, and this belief, whatever it is, touches the right physiological triggers and levers to make them happen. If there were no belief—if the organism did not falsely attribute to the placebo the power to bring about a physiological change—there would be no placebo.

All placebos are mind-body phenomena. Several analysts of placebos have made the case that at least one important source of placebos—that is, of the belief that allows something to be a placebo—is conditioning.

Take a simple, frequently used example. A child is repeatedly made well by a man wearing a white medical jacket. This happens periodically as the child grows up. When the child is an adult and goes to a doctor's office for medical help, the sight of a man in a white medical jacket brings a degree of immediate relief. The early experiences have led the child to make an association between men with white medical jackets and an improvement in health. The man in the white jacket became the medicine just as, for Ader and Cohen's rats, the saccharin-flavored liquid became an immune suppressant.

The process that makes this possible is conditioning. Just as Pavlov taught his dog to respond to a bell as if it were food, just as Ader and Cohen taught their rats to respond to a sugary drink as if it were an immune-suppressing drug, so undirected and uncoordinated experiences—life as the child lived it—taught the child to respond to the man wearing a white medical jacket as if this constellation was the medicine that brought relief.

Conditioning may not be the only source of placebos, but it is clearly a major source. Ader makes the point more compactly in the title of one of his papers, "The Placebo Effect as a Conditioned Response." Conditioning is a source of placebos, and conditioned responses are placebos.

But all such analysis, as Ader explains, is only analysis. For researchers of mind-body phenomena, there has been no way to study placebos concretely, in the laboratory. In a sense, the means to make and study placebos experimentally have existed ever since Pavlov got his dog to salivate at the sound of a bell. The bell is a placebo, and this experiment may be the first unassailable laboratory proof that the mind can move the body. But for whatever reason, and despite the recognition that placebos can be created in life by conditioning, Ader appears to be the first person to make the connection between the familiar laboratory creation of conditioned responses and the only vaguely understood phenomenon of placebos.

Ader and Cohen's work now provides a precise method to create placebos and to test them. How Ader will use these methods and his analysis of placebos as conditioned responses will depend on his interests. One possibility he has discussed is developing placebos to be used as part of a drug-and-placebo regime, and he has initiated several studies (and written some theoretical papers) examining how this might be done. The larger point is that such studies can now take place because Ader realized he was a man who could make placebos in the laboratory.

Ader's Achievement and the Conditioned "Mind"

What Neal Miller did for the autonomic nervous system, Ader has done for the immune system: uncovered its integral attachment to the essential processes by which an organism sorts out the flow of experience, gives it shape, and incorporates it into the activities of the physical body. Ader's work should help close the door on studies of the body that isolate any bodily system from the world of experience within which a body lives. Ader's achievement is large. It should recast the study of immunology. It has reshaped the landscape of mind-body research. It is now possible to explore freshly, and with new confidence, the connections between the mind (the collector and sorter of experience) and the development of infectious disease, the illnesses that for nearly a century have been ascribed primarily to pathogens. This possibility, in turn, may (or may not) weaken the prevalent unexamined presumption that the source of all disorders, even mental disorders, will ultimately turn out to be identifiable physical entities.

Yet it can also be said—the refrain has probably become familiar—that the "mind" in Ader and Cohen's conditioning studies, like the separate "minds" of Type A, the relaxation response, and biofeedback, is not a "mind" that knows what it is doing. If the "mind" of biofeedback is a "trial-and-error mind," the "mind" of the conditioning studies is one of "rote learning." The rat knows how to suppress its immune system—or else it could not do it. But it does not put this knowledge into action of its own volition. The rat has been tricked by the techniques of conditioning. The rat's experience has been manipulated so that the rat—without deliberation, without a decision, without a recognition that another possibility exists—automatically does what it knows how to do.

Of course a rat may not have volition, may not be able to deliberate, make a decision, or recognize alternatives. But that is the point. Without any of these capacities, the "mind" that it exercises in the conditioning studies can still alter immune reactions.

That human beings are capable of exercising the same sort of mindless "mind" is unquestionable. We have all been conditioned in some ways by life and experience, and the results can sometimes be physiologically detrimental. The "mind" that the rat uses exists, and it exists in us too. It is one more kind of "mind" that can move the body, but it is not a mind that of its own accord tells the body to move.

CHAPTER 5

Candace Pert
and the Swarming Neuropeptides

I⊤ is not surprising in an area as young as the study of mind and body that investigators trying to discover how the mind might talk with the body should come upon new phenomena, even, perhaps, entirely new body systems. If the body is presumed to live its life mostly apart from the mind, no one bothers to explore the mechanics of their possible connections. But once it appears that the mind is in contact with the body, the mechanics become important, and researchers begin to look at details and phenomena that earlier had seemed unimportant. Such concentrated observation will almost always lead to the uncovering of new details and new phenomena, which in turn lead to more. Suddenly, pathways in the body that were once thought to be as empty and uninviting as a dark alley are as alive as a disco dance floor after midnight.

Something like this has happened in investigations of the former no-man's-land between the central nervous system and the immune system. Researchers have turned up new functions for familiar hormones, new neural connections between the two systems, and new immune-related activities of a class of chemical substances, called neurotransmitters, which serve the purpose of carrying information across the gap that separates nerve cells.

Very few investigators of the physiological mechanisms that might serve as links in a chain between mind and body make an effort to understand the practical significance of new findings. They merely offer the findings (whose ferreting out often demands ingenuity and a high degree of technical skill) as further evidence of one or another mind (brain)-body connection. The needs of mind or body that the connection might serve, the experience, emotion, or desire that might initiate the connection—such matters are issues that their findings cannot address (for all intents and purposes the findings are treated like data describing the working of an intricate, exotic, and inanimate mechanism), and the investigators rarely choose to speculate on them.

Candace Pert, a biochemist, is an exception. Pert studies neuropeptides—the chemicals produced by nerve cells in the brain (though it appears that they may also be produced by nerve cells elsewhere)—and the receptors into which they (like any other bodily or manufactured chemical) must fit to do their work.

About 60 neuropeptides have been identified so far (they are distinguished from one another by their amino acids), and every neuropeptide (every bodily chemical, every drug) has its own type of receptor. No neuropeptide can use the receptor of another neuropeptide. No receptor can accommodate the neuropeptide of another receptor. The image commonly used to describe the relationship between a neuropeptide (any chemical) and its receptor is the image of a key and a lock. The neuropeptide is the key, the receptor, which apparently sits on the surface of a cell, is the lock, and unless the right key is in the right lock, nothing happens: The specific action "sought" by the neuropeptide is thwarted.

Since neuropeptides come (usually) from the brain, they are obvious candidates for the role of brain messengers, and a good deal of work has been done on their structure and on the variety of activities they start or stop or otherwise regulate. The emphasis in these studies is more on the neuropeptides than on the receptors.

Pert has taken another tack. The receptors are what fascinate her, particularly their distribution. With new techniques that she has helped develop, Pert and her associates have discovered that receptors for all the identified neuropeptides are concentrated in specific areas in the brain and the rest of the body. Pert calls the areas "nodal points" or "hot spots." These findings are new data: Pert and her associates have detailed them in several highly technical papers. They are information about the body that no one knew before.

Most researchers of the mechanics of the body usually stop at the documentation of new data. Pert, with her colleagues, has gone further, to fashion a striking new theory about the mechanics of mind-body interaction. Pert believes that the mind talks to the body using neuropeptides, and uses neuropeptides and their receptors to organize and integrate—"prioritize" is a word she sometimes uses—the internal life of the body.

Pert has only lightly alluded to this theory in her professional papers, but she has felt comfortable explaining it in presentations to both professional and lay audiences. Two of these talks have been published, and the boldest, in which she refers to the possibility that the mind may "survive the death of the physical brain," has been reprinted several times in publications aimed at people who like to entertain new ideas and believe that there may be more to the mind than the body. If there is a biochemist of the "new age," it is Pert.

The Lure of the Opiate Receptor

The journey that brought Pert to the new world of neuropeptides and their receptors began in 1972, in the second year of Richard Nixon's "war on drugs." Pert was a Ph.D. student at Johns Hopkins University, in the laboratory of Solomon Snyder. In the 1960s, Snyder, a psychiatrist and neuroscientist, had been among the first researchers to show that psychiatric disorders were also chemical imbalances and could be treated chemically. (Most researchers of mind-body phenoma want to establish the mind's effect on the body. Snyder had taken the opposite approach: to establish the body's effect on the mind. Mental disorders, as he saw them, were essentially matters of disturbed chemistry, not of disturbed thinking and feeling.) Pert looked to Snyder as a mentor. She already had a grand ambition to discover the chemistry of the emotions. Pert was an English major before becoming a biochemist, and she often approaches science with what literary critics call a romantic sensibility. Snyder's accomplishment in revealing the chemistry of mental disorders was for her a powerful entry into the scientific territory she wanted to explore.

When Pert joined Snyder's lab, he gave her a fairly mechanical project—to determine whether the amount of chemical that a cell pulled into itself by a special pumping action was related to the creation of another chemical. The project was a solid subject for a Ph.D. thesis, but according to Snyder, Pert "set no world records for enthusiasm or experimental progress."

She had been working on the project for several months when Snyder received a government grant to conduct basic research on opiate addiction. The grant was part of the Nixon war-on-drugs program that had been announced the year before in response to public alarm over the growing use of opiates in the United States and among the soldiers in Vietnam. Most of the funds allocated to the war on drugs was used to develop drug-treatment programs, but a portion of the money was designated for basic research.

Snyder had received funds for two research projects. In one project, which consituted the bulk of the grant, he would extend his previous research on the brain chemicals involved in the effects of amphetamines, a drug of choice among certain segments of the population. In the other project, he would make an effort to isolate what was called the opiate receptor. Whether there was such a thing no one knew for a fact.

It had long been assumed that every chemical drug produced its effects on the body by entering a cell through a sort of portal that conformed to the shape of the drug molecule. This portal, for obvious reasons, was called a receptor. In the instance of opiate drugs, the case for the existence of receptors was especially strong. Receptors would explain why some opiates were more potent than other opiates. (If each opiate had its own receptor, and different opiates had different numbers of receptors, then the opiates with the most receptors would have the most potency.) Receptors would also explain why certain drugs, called antagonists, could block the effects of an opiate in a matter of minutes. (Presumably the antagonist was filling up the receptor, preventing the opiate from getting in.)

The person who discovered the opiate receptor would clearly score a major scientific coup. The discovery would open a new door on the understanding of how opiates work, and it could be an important step in the medical control of addiction.

When Snyder received his grant, he decided not to pursue his study of amphetamines. He was becoming bored with that avenue of research, he has explained, and he decided to use all the grant money to search for the opiate receptor. He told Pert to put away her work on the pumping action project, and with him as her supervisor—everything about this research had to be devised—they would try to tease out the opiate receptor.

Initial Failures, and at Last Success

The committee reviewing Snyder's grant proposal had described his project on the opiate receptor as risky, a "flyer," and had reduced the sum of money that he had asked to allocated to it. What Snyder and Pert wanted to do was a long shot. Simply put, they were looking for a piece of the body that conceivably did not exist and that no one had isolated before because no one knew how to. Since the brain had to be the location of opiate receptors (the behavioral changes associated with opiates necessarily had their source in alterations in the brain), Snyder and Pert had to find a way to chop up the brain so that only opiate receptors—and not the receptors for anything else—rose to the top like cream.

Drawing on techniques developed by researchers who two years earlier had found the receptors of several hormones (in areas such as the liver and muscles, not in the brain) and on elements of an unsuccessful approach to isolate the opiate receptor (by a leading pharmacological researcher, Avrum Goldstein), Snyder and Pert put together a complex strategy. Pert first homogenized the brains of rats, guinea pigs, or mice and then took an opiate that had been "tagged" with a radioactive element and, in effect, stirred it into the soup-like brain liquid. The radioactivity would function like a little spotlight. Whenever an opiate bound to something, there would be a light of radioactivity. With the aid of several other techniques, it was possible to "count" the number of lights.

But Pert and Snyder knew that some of the lights would not represent receptor bindings. Like any chemical substance, opiates can bind to a variety of items, to fat cells, for example. They can also be caught between cells. When such bindings occurred, the opiates, of course, would have no effect. But to an observer of homogenized brain cells, there would be no way of distinguishing a receptor binding from any other kind of binding.

To deal with the problem of excluding nonreceptor bindings, Pert prepared another batch of brain-cell liquid with a radioactively tagged opiate, but this time she also stirred in a second type of opiate that was not radioactively tagged. A distinguishing characteristic of the second opiate was that it could edge out the first in binding to the opiate receptor. In effect, the faster-acting, nonvisible opiate would fill up the opiate receptors before the slower-acting visible opiate got to them. Any visible bindings, then, would be nonreceptor bindings.

In practice, the rest of the experiment amounted to arithmetic. Since the visible bindings in the first batch of brain cells included both true receptor bindings and other types of bindings, while the visible bindings in the second batch essentially constituted nonreceptor bindings, the number of visible bindings in the first batch—legitimate and irrelevant—minus the number of visible bindings in the second batch—only irrelevant—would equal true receptor bindings and nothing else.

This was the plan, but it did not work. Pert, who did the experiments, found no appreciable difference in the count between the first and second batches. She spent weeks trying to fine-tune the details. According to Snyder, "Candace tried valiantly to modify the experimental conditions. . . . All to no avail."

Snyder was inclined to call a halt. If an experiment did not swiftly give up its findings or seem to promise that it might, he preferred to move on. There was also the problem of Pert's Ph.D. If the receptor project came to nothing, which is certainly how it seemed, then Pert's time would have been lost, and she would have to start over on something else.

Pert suggested that they try another approach. Before, she

had radioactively tagged an opiate. What if, instead, she tagged a chemical antagonist—a substance that blocked the opiate from producing its effects, presumably because the antagonist beat the opiate to the receptor. Perhaps an antagonist would bind to the opiate receptors in the brain-cell solution in larger numbers than the opiate she was using. Snyder thought it was worth a try, and he and Pert decided to use the common antagonist naloxone (which is routinely used to prevent deaths from drug overdose).

A few more weeks went by. The results were fundamentally no different. As far as Snyder was concerned, it was now time to stop. He told Pert to end the project, and he put her back on the earlier pumping study. He did it "out of compassion," Pert has said. "He thought I would never get my Ph.D."

Without telling Snyder, Pert tried the experiment again. And this time, for the first time, there was a clear and substantial difference in the number of bindings in the two batches of brain cells, and the difference represented bindings to an opiate receptor. Pert and Snyder were sure that they had succeeded.

To test the finding, Pert used different opiates with naloxone and achieved comparable results. She got good results using intestinal material instead of brain material (opiates have an effect on the intestines). Then, when she used chemicals that were not opiates, she got no results—a confirmation that the experiment had isolated bindings to an opiate receptor and not to anything else.

She was also able to show that the receptor count corresponded to the potency of an opiate. The stronger the opiate, the higher the count. All the pieces fit.

In March 1973, Pert and Snyder's paper on their findings appeared in *Science* magazine. Pert was listed as the first author, an unusual honor for a Ph.D. student working in the laboratory of the second author. The government, which was not winning many battles in either the war on drugs or in Vietnam, was happy to arrange a press conference on the day of the article's publication. Both Snyder and Pert were present to discuss the findings. The story received wide attention, not always for the right reasons. "Cocaine Cure Discovered by Hopkins Researchers," one headline declared. "I was struck," Snyder commented, "by the extraordinary capacity of the news media to misinterpret stories."

Pert and Snyder later learned that their first experiments had failed because they were using a light-sensitive opiate that had been deactivated by the fluorescent lights in the lab.

The Discovery of Endorphins

Since the brain contained an opiate receptor, it followed that the brain must have its own opiate-like substances. The brain could not reasonably have a receptor simply for the chance possibility that a poppy-derived substance would make use of it. The receptor had to be there for something made by the brain itself, a natural opiate.

Even before the discovery of the opiate receptor by Snyder and Pert, the strong likelihood that it existed had already spurred two laboratories—one in Aberdeen, Scotland, one in California—to try and isolate the natural opiate that belonged to it. When Snyder and Pert announced that they had found the opiate receptor, it became clear that it was only a matter of time before someone would find the natural opiate it existed to receive. The two laboratories already working on the project and a number of others (including Snyder's) now joined a search that was the scientific equivalent of a hundred-yard dash.

The discovery came relatively quickly, and not in Snyder's lab. In December 1975, slightly less than three years after Snyder and Pert had identified the opiate receptor, two researchers from Aberdeen, Scotland, Hans Kosterlitz and John Hughes, laid claim to discovering the first opiate-like substance of the brain. Chemically, they reported, it was like morphine—which, in molecular terms, meant that it was a peptide, an example of the class of chemical substances, neuropeptides, that would soon occupy Pert's attention.

Other discoveries of opiate-like peptide substances—generically called opioids, to distinguish them from opiates—were announced in the next several years. By mid-1979, over a half dozen opioids had been isolated. The brain, it seems, is an opioid factory. As the number of opioids grew, each of which had its own name, they collectively become known as endorphins, a contraction of the words "endogenous," meaning internal, and "morphine."

The discovery of endorphins gave mind-body research a new twist. Everyone knew that the brain stimulated by a particular chemical, could set loose a cascade of events that would finally conclude in altering one or another physiological process. Now it was clear that the brain itself could manufacture such substances, that the brain could make biochemicals that would bring large bodily changes in "tone" and "feeling"—the relief of pain, the relief of fatigue, a feeling of energy. But the question of exactly what experience, emotion, feeling, mental technique, or mental association might cause the brain to manufacture and release its endorphins, this critical question was outside the interests of the people who had uncovered the endorphins, just as a comparable question was outside the interests of most of the people identifying the material bits and pieces that link the brain to the rest of the body.

Pert, meanwhile, had taken a position in the brain chemistry section of the National Institute of Mental Health (after receiving her Ph.D.) and also continued working with Snyder, investigating receptors. Then, an accolade given to Snyder but not to Pert for the opiate receptor work in which she assumed she had been a full partner—symbolized by the fact that she was listed as the first author of the article in which she and Snyder announced their findings—severed their relationship.

In November 1978, Snyder, along with Hans Kosterlitz and John Hughes (who had discovered the first endorphin), were given the United States' most prestigious scientific award, the Albert and Mary Lasker Award, for their work in discovering and investigating the opiate receptor and the brain's own opiates. Pert was furious about her exclusion and, untypical of the social customs of the scientific community, was public about her anger. The episode became a cause célèbre. In the end, nothing changed. The award was given to Snyder, Kosterlitz, and Hughes, and not to Pert.

That the episode still rankles, at least for Snyder and Pert and their immediate circles, is clear from Snyder's memoir-like history of the opiate receptor work and the discoveries to which it led. The book *Brainstorming* was published in 1989, 11 years after he won the Lasker Award. Snyder fully describes the work for which he received the award, but does not mention winning it.

Mapping Receptors in the Brain

One of the projects that Pert worked on in Snyder's lab after she and Snyder had found the opiate receptor was to isolate the receptors of other natural chemical substances of the brain. She concentrated on neurotransmitters, the chemical substances that are produced by brain neurons and that "transmit" information across the slight gap—called a synapse—that separates nerve cell from adjoining nerve cell and nerve cell from adjoining muscles.

Neurotransmitters play key roles in regulating the internal physiology of the body. Norepinephrine, for example, is a neurotransmitter that can constrict the small blood vessels, slow the heart rate, raise the blood pressure, and relax the smooth muscles of the intestinal tract. Some neurotransmitters also appear to be involved in mental and nervous disorders such as schizophrenia and Alzheimer's disease.

In a rush of activity, Pert, using the receptor-isolating techniques that she had developed with Snyder, identified one neurotransmitter receptor after another. She also began "mapping" the location of the receptors. She looked at the brain first. Where in the brain were the entry points that allowed the chemicals of the brain to do their work in regulating the physiology of the body?

To find out, she developed another new technique, this time with a research colleague in Snyder's lab, Michael Kuhar. Called autoradiography, the technique essentially amounts to taking a cross-section slice of the brain, sprinkling it with radioactively labeled substances that stick to a particular receptor, and placing the brain slice on top of a sheet of film where the radioactive material imprints itself. This is done for all the receptors. The result is a "map" of the distribution of receptors in the brain.

She soon saw that the distribution formed a pattern. Already in 1974, at a meeting at which the Aberdeen researcher John Hughes first announced that he and Hans Kosterlitz were on the track of a morphine-like substance in the brain, Pert was able to report that there was a surprisingly high density of receptors in the part of the brain called the limbic system.

The limbic system is among the least understood sections of the brain. While its full function is not known, it includes two structures (the pituitary gland and the hypothalamus) which between them regulate and coordinate, among other things, the hormonal activity of the body and the activities of the autonomic nervous system. Most centrally, and most important for Pert, the limbic system is strongly involved—no one is sure how—in the expression and perhaps the creation of emotion.

That an area of the brain was intimately connected with emotion was first learned from experiments that neurologists conducted in the 1920s on conscious men and women. The neurologists electrically stimulated an area of the brain located above a structure called the amygdala (which is involved with anger and sexual behavior) and found that they could evoke "a whole gamut of emotional display," as Pert describes the result. There were "powerful reactions of grief, of pain, of pleasure associated with profound memories." Along with these emotions was "the total somatic accompaniment of emotional states."

Could it be mere coincidence that the part of the brain that regulated much of the physiology of the body, that was intimately associated with emotion also housed dense concentrations of receptors?

As the brain's opioids were isolated, Pert identified and located their receptors, and again found concentrations in the limbic system.

She began to look for receptors outside the brain and found a concentration in a part of the spinal cord (which, with the brain, forms the central nervous system) called the dorsal horn. The dorsal horn is the entry point for all incoming sensory information—sight, sound, smell, touch, taste. The information is then sent to the brain.

Pert now had two striking pieces of new information. Receptors for the brain chemicals that regulated much of the physiology of the body were concentrated in the area of the brain that dealt with emotions. A concentration of receptors for the same chemicals also existed in the area of the spinal cord that was the entry point for all sensory information.

To Pert and her associates, when these two findings were put together, they revealed the purpose of receptors and why they are where they are and why the regulatory structures of the body are where they are. The argument goes like this: A person is regularly bombarded by sensory information. It comes pouring in an indiscriminate rush through the dorsal horn and must be dealt with in triage-like fashion. Some of it must be acted on, some must be discarded, all of it must be ordered according to its urgency and importance. What orders the information, Pert believes, is emotion. There are receptors in the limbic system and the dorsal horn (which Pert and her colleagues believe should be seen as part of the limbic system) because the emotions associated with the limbic system mobilize a "chemical system to prioritize all this information" coming in through the dorsal horn.

"Put simply," Pert has said, "your emotions tell you what to do," and the receptors put the message into practice.

When Pert was asked to give a talk to lay people at the National Institutes of Health in 1981 to explain in general terms the meaning of her work, she called the talk "Brain Receptors for Opiates and Other Psychoactive Drugs," and she used the subtitle to indicate the significance that she and her colleagues saw in the data they had been collecting: "Keys to the Biochemistry of Emotion."

The Integrated Receptor Network

By 1985, Pert and her colleagues were ready to take the argument further. In a highly technical presentation of their work in the *Journal of Immunology*, she again looked to an elaboration of the paper's title to point to the significance of the findings. The paper was called "Neuropeptides and Their Receptors: A Psychosomatic Network." Pert had come to the view that receptors and the substances that bound to them constituted a broad network linking mind and body.

The primary basis of the enlarged view is more receptor mappings. Pert and her colleagues had found receptors in areas well outside of the brain and the spinal cord. They had found a sizable cluster of receptors in the intestine. They had found an opiate receptor in the gonads and a receptor for a neurotransmitter in the kidneys. Most strikingly, they had found a cluster of receptors on an immune cell called a monocyte, which performs many health-sustaining activities in the body.

These were Pert's findings as of 1985. There likely were other receptors in the same areas, and perhaps in other areas as well. Basically, her findings represented the receptors she had looked for. As of 1987, for example, she and her colleagues had searched the surface of the monocyte cell looking for six receptors, and they had found all six.

For Pert and her colleagues, these findings indicated that neuropeptides and their receptors form a bodywide network. The receptors were not only in the brain, affecting the endocrine system (and thus the hormonal regulators of the body) and in the spinal cord, where sensory information entered the body; they were also in the gastrointestinal system, the reproductive system (the opiate receptor in the gonads), and the immune system. This could not just be a random strewing of receptors here and there. To Pert, the receptors are where they are to organize and integrate the activities of the body in response to the brain's dictates that come in the form of neuropeptides.

To illustrate what she means when she says that receptors integrate the activities and responses of the body, she uses data from studies by other researchers on a neuropeptide called angiotension. One study found that when angiotensin is injected into the brain of a rat that had been allowed to sate its thirst completely, the rat will begin to drink again in about 30 seconds. Another study found that when agiotensin is injected into a rat's kidney, the kidney shuts down in a way that prevents the rat from losing liquid.

In Pert's view, these two responses complement each other. Angiotensin in the brain makes the rat act to quench a thirst; angiotensin in the kidney makes the rat conserve the liquid it has. A thirsty rat obviously would want to do both things simultaneously. For Pert, the presence of the angiotensin receptor in both brain and kidney shows that the body is prepared to act in an integrated way—and that the receptors integrate it. The angiotensin receptors only await the angiotensin to direct the body to drink and to conserve the liquid in the body.

So-called gut feelings provide Pert with a more anecdotal example. Gut feelings are commonly regarded as a subjective phenomenon, a kind of imagining of the mind that somehow turns up in the stomach. For Pert, they are an objective biological experience. People have gut feelings, she maintains, because they have receptors in the intestines. The neuropeptide that snaps into the receptors comes from the brain, but the feeling it creates is in the gut.

To Pert, receptors in a sense house the mind (or brain). As long as a gut feeling lasts, for example, the mind (or brain) can be said to be in the gut. "The brain is certainly important," she once told an audience. "It's right up there with your spleen"—which is dense with receptors.

It is critical to Pert's theory that receptors can be found on the monocyte cell of the immune system. If receptors are the key to integrating mind and body, they must be part of the body's primary defense system against invading pathogens, otherwise it makes little sense to speak of integration. There could be no integrated response in the body if the immune system were not also part of what Pert calls "the neuropeptide network."

How Pert's work fits with Ader's examination of the immune system is not easy to say. It may be that neuropeptides and their receptors could help explain the results of Ader's conditioning studies, but this is not a foregone conclusion. It is also not clear how a process like conditioning—essentially a learning process— connects with Pert's idea that emotions are the phenomena that push neuropeptides into action. All that is clear is that both Pert and Ader are persuaded, with different kinds of evidence as support, that the brain "talks" to the immune system.

106

What makes the monocyte cell so interesting and formidable an element of the immune system is that the cell travels through the body on the watch for alien bacteria. (It has other functions too.) When a monocyte finds such bacteria, it produces another type of immune cell, a macrophage, which has the task of destroying the bacteria, essentially by engulfing it and eating it up.

In studies of the monocyte, one of Pert's colleagues, Michael Rull, has found, remarkably, that neuropeptides can act as signals to attract monocytes. The neuropeptides send out a "call," and the monocytes move toward them in response. The neuropeptides function as a kind of radar guiding the movement of the monocyte. In effect, the brain sends out neuropeptides, which then send for the monocytes, which bring within them the bacteria-devouring macrophages.

The integrating property of receptors is confirmed for Pert by the fact that the neuropeptides travel in the blood and do not use the one-place-at-a-time "hard-wiring" of the nerve cells. Neuropeptides enter the blood and go where they need to go, to all their receptors at the same time. They are not caught in the lock-step of linear movement, which first must touch point A before it can touch point B and only then can touch point C. Neuropeptides can touch all three points simultaneously, an obvious need if a system is to integrate the activities of a body. Pert sometimes calls neuropeptides "neurojuices," to convey her sense of how they stream through the blood, as in a kind of flood.

The Role of Emotion and the Neuropeptide "Mind"

For Pert, the mobilizing force behind neuropeptides, sending them to their appropriate receptors, is emotion. Pert has not made clear what she means by emotion. She sometimes talks

107

about "mood" or "tone." She suggests that breathing, as practiced by yogis and by women in labor, can bring about a kind of "mood" state that can, in laboring women for example, relieve pain. Breathing, in this sequence, becomes a move toward emotion. In the example concerning the neuropeptide angiotensin, thirst seems to function as an emotion.

None of Pert's remarks about emotion are more than remarks. As with other investigators of the physical mechanisms that might link mind and body, her primary focus, despite her large vision, is on the mechanisms—in her case, on an integrated system of neuropeptides and receptors that starts, so to speak, in the emotion-laden mysterious limbic system of the brain.

Pert's view of mind-body interactions has a touch of grandeur. Neuropeptides rush in a flood everywhere to energize receptors brilliantly placed so that the body in one swirling movement reorders itself perfectly to meet the challenge of a moment, and then does it again and again. But what might start this all-at-once reordering--an emotion, a mood, a tone—is as mechanical as the entrance of angiotensin into its receptor.

The "mind" of this body is a "mind" that acts automatically. In this respect, it is like the "mind" of the relaxation response. An emotion (mood, tone) registers, and the emotion instantaneously picks the neuropeptides that the emotion, for whatever reason, needs. The "mind" has an endless repertoire of such regulating manipulations, but the manipulations have nothing to do with the explicit wishes of the organism on whose behalf they are made. The organism does not know these manipulations are taking place. They happen by themselves.

CHAPTER 6

Theodore Barber
and the Royal Road of "Hypnosis"

THEODORE Barber is a psychologist and researcher who has spent much of his professional career examining and analyzing the phenomenon of hypnosis. He was drawn to the study of hypnosis when he was a graduate student in the 1950s and read in the *British Medical Journal* a case report by a doctor who had used hypnosis to help a 16-year-old boy clear up about 70 percent of a congenital and progressively worsening skin condition that other doctors had declared incurable and untreatable.

"When I first read Mason's paper," Barber wrote a half-century later, "I found it difficult to believe; it was saying unequivocally that by guiding a person to feel-think-imagine in a new way about his/her abnormal skin, new normal skin forms step by step with the guided feeling-thinking-imagining." The report had a catalytic effect on Barber. "I already was deeply involved in trying to understand the mind-body problem; Mason's report was the final, determining factor which led me to decide to devote my efforts to understanding hypnosis, since it indicated that the royal road to solving the mind-body problem involved unraveling the mystery of hypnosis."

That royal road, for Barber, has not been entirely straight. To most academicians involved in hypnosis, its essential characteristic is that it constitutes a unique state of consciousness approximating a trance. This trance state, in their view, is not a chance event. It is brought about by a special technique called an induction procedure ("you are becoming drowsy, your eyelids feel heavy," and so forth). Further, in the trance state—susceptibility to being hypnotized varies, and not everyone can achieve the trance state or enter it as fully—people generally have capacities that are not available to them in the normal waking state: They become immune to certain kinds of pain, their limbs take on an extreme heaviness, they will forget something that occurred in the hypnotic state when they are instructed to do so. In this traditional understanding of the special character of hypnosis, there is little or no interest in using hypnosis as the English doctor used it—to heal a physical disorder.

Barber had a different view of hypnosis. He saw it as a heightened state of what he calls suggestion, not as a unique state of consciousness that must be triggered by a special induction procedure. By "suggestion," Barber means a state in which individuals give full credence to statements they hear about themselves and their capacities. Barber uses the word suggestion in the same sense that one says some people are "suggestible"—they believe whatever they hear. Hypnosis, says Barber, is such a state of suggestibility, which obviously can occur under many circumstances of ordinary life.

For perhaps the first 20 years of his career, Barber conducted a running debate with the scholarly hypnosis community on the question of whether hypnosis is any different from suggestion. He has critiqued the studies that lay claim to finding such differences, and he has conducted his own research to show that suggestion and hypnosis can usually accomplish the same results.

The debate often spins on details and sometimes seems to be about nothing other than itself. But it involves an important issue. If hypnosis and suggestion are roughly the same, then the state of being "hypnotized" is a far more common event in everyday life than most people realize and the phenomena experienced under hypnosis, which are presumed to be solely the product of hypnosis, are actually phenomena that are present in everyday life. In this debate, the defenders of hypnosis as a unique state of consciousness represent the elitists and Barber represents the populist upstart, claiming hypnosis/suggestion for everyone.

Only after many years of involvement in the issue of hypnosis versus suggestion did Barber more actively pursue the interest that brought him to hypnosis: the mind-body problem. (He seems to have been stimulated by the emergence of the biofeedback "movement," in which he became a participant, and its focus on self-regulation.) Barber's approach centered on the gradual compilation and deepening analysis of a series of widely diverse studies showing the capacity of people under hypnosis or suggestion to alter bodily processes. The most extensive form of this compilation, published in 1984, appeared in the long review and analysis that stimulated my own efforts to understand what the study of mind and body was all about—"Changing 'Unchangeable' Bodily Processes by (Hypnotic) Suggestions: A New Look at Hypnosis, Cognitions, Imagining, and the Mind-Body Problem."

What Barber accomplishes in this survey is to show in close up, as if the paper were a film documentary, a remarkable assortment of people who succeeded in altering, partially or wholly, particular body conditions that they had set their minds to change. For these people, there was no mind–body problem. There was only a dramatically direct way of dealing with the body.

The two "parts" of Barber's career have a clear link. If suggestions can do what hypnosis can, then the bodily changes achieved under hypnosis are likely to be possible under the much more common condition of suggestion. Studies in Barber's paper show that this is so. You do not need to be hypnotized to use your mind to move your body.

Hypnosis vs. Suggestion

In his research comparing hypnosis with suggestion, Barber usually divides his subjects into two groups. One group is hypnotized with the standard hypnotic induction procedure, while the other group hears a set of comments encouraging them to believe in the suggestions they will soon receive (for example, "Research studies have shown that ordinary people can . . ."). The two groups are then each given the same suggestion/directive to display one or more of the characteristics that presumably distinguishes the hypnotic state from all other states of consciousness, such as forgetting what one has been told to forget or feeling no pain when putting one's finger into icy water.

Barber regularly finds that both groups react similarly to the directive. The group that is simply told to believe in the suggestions displays the same amount of "hypnotic" behavior as the hypnotized group. Both groups have the same percentage of people who succeed in forgetting what they are told to forget or who report no pain when they put their fingers into icy water. At times, the suggestion group even shows a greater amount of "hypnotic" behavior than the hypnotized group, with more people doing what the researcher suggests they do.

Barber's most comprehensive comparative study of hypnosis and suggestion appeared in 1977, in a paper called "Hypnosis, Suggestion, and Altered States of Consciousness" in *Annals of the New York Academy of Sciences.* Barber, with

112

Sheryl Wilson, divided 66 participants into three equal groups. One group received a standard hypnotic induction, a second group received what Barber calls "think-with instructions" (encouraging the subjects to go along with and accept the forthcoming suggestions), and the third group, the control group, was told only that it was part of a study. All three groups were then tested for their ability to perform or experience 10 phenomena that are taken to be standard manifestations of the so-called hypnotic trance state—phenomena such as arm heaviness, the ability to remember experiences and feelings from an earlier time in one's life (age regression, in the parlance of hypnosis), and finger anesthesia.

Barber and Wilson found that the people who received the "think-with instructions" did the best. They "obtained significantly higher scores . . . than those exposed to the traditional trance-induction procedure or the control treatment." Barber and Wilson also reported that they achieved the same result in two other studies. In both, the subjects who were "randomly assigned to a 'think-with instructions' treatment were more responsive to test suggestions than those randomly assigned to a traditional trance-induction treatment."

These findings, Barber and Wilson maintained, supported two propositions. They indicated that suggestion is as powerful as hypnosis and that hypnosis itself is a way of thinking about and responding to experience. Like suggestion, hypnosis is a "cognitive-behavioral" phenomenon—a way of thinking, in this case with willing acceptance—and not a trance state.

Proponents of the trance-state view of hypnosis have generally countered Barber's research with one of two arguments. One argument contends that the people given instructions to think in a certain way are in fact hypnotized—that Barber ends up comparing hypnotized people with hypnotized people. This, of course, is possible. But if it is true, it means, at the very least, that the traditional trance induction is not needed to hypnotize people, a possibility that, in turn, would suggest that the hypnotic state is more common than ordinarily presumed.

The other argument contends that Barber's studies are not a true test of hypnosis because hypnosis can be tested only among people who are susceptible to it, and since Barber randomly assigns his subjects to one or another treatment group, he likely includes people in the hypnotized group who are not fully susceptible to hypnosis. The argument is plausible (especially if one believes in the uniqueness of the hypnotic state), but the few studies that have tried to confirm it have failed.

Barber and his supporters have trained their own criticism on the research claiming to provide evidence that hypnosis constitutes a trance-like state of consciousness. To Barber and his supporters, virtually all such studies are fundamentally flawed because they do not include a suggestion group. The studies simply take the trance view of hypnosis for granted and then present the out-of-the-ordinary behavior of its hypnotized subjects as proof of the uniqueness of the hypnotic state.

Barber and his supporters have also been able to use as ammunition the studies in which the proponents of the trance view have tried to identify the physiological characteristics that distinguish the hypnotic state from the normal state of wakefulness (as Herbert Benson and R. Keith Wallace were able to identify the physiological differences that distinguished meditation from sitting quietly or sleeping). There have been many such studies, but no distinguishing characteristics have been found. If hypnosis is unique, Barber asks, why does there appear to be nothing physiologically unique about it?

In terms of a clear-cut resolution, this debate has not come to an end so much as it has stopped. The arguments have been made, and the evidence has been presented; the elitists hold to their view, and the populists to theirs. But short of a conclusion, Barber's assault on the trance-state view of hypnosis has convinced its advocates that suggestion may be a component in at least some of the phenomena that have been distinctly associated with hypnosis and, accordingly, that some phenomena of hypnosis may be present in the ordinary nonhypnotic currents of everyday life.

Some Remarkable Case Studies

Reading Barber's "Changing 'Unchangeable' Bodily Processes by (Hypnotic) Suggestions" is a little like reading a domesticated version of the stories on the front pages of sensationalistic tabloids. The paper contains a parade of people who apparently did no more than use their minds to alter one or another response or process of their bodies. Again and again, thoughts and imaginings seem to be the source of precise and sometimes profound physical changes. In these examples, the heavy body seems about as responsive to the insubstantial mind as a trained dog is to its master.

For Barber, the single most powerful example of the mind's direct capacity to alter the physiological processes of the body is the case that initially drew him to the study of hypnosis: the achievement of the English doctor who used hypnosis to help the 16-year-old boy with an increasingly offensive and constraining congenital skin disease restore some 70 percent of his afflicted skin. At the time of treatment, the boy's hands, arms, back, buttocks, thighs, legs, and feet were covered with scaly, dark-colored, and hardened skin. He was suffering from congenital ichthyosiform erythrodermis, colloquially called "fish-skin disease."

The disease had become severe. The boy's skin "was about as hard as normal fingernails, was numb for a depth of several millimeters, and was so inelastic that attempts at bending would produce cracks in the surface which would then ooze blood-stained serum." The scaly skin had also become a breeding ground for bacteria, "which caused a putrid odor," and the boy no longer attended school because the teachers' and students' objected to the odor.

There is no known cause for fish-skin disease and no known treatment. It is regarded as incurable, and various doctors were unsuccessful in their efforts to help the boy with different salves.

In the boy's first session under hypnosis, the doctor, A. A. Mason, told him to focus on his left arm and "to feel the skin becoming normal." In five days, the hardened layer of skin on the left arm softened and fell off.

In sessions over the next several weeks, Mason continued to tell the boy to focus on a particular area of his body and to feel the skin in that area becoming normal. The improvements were dramatic and rapid. Both arms cleared, 90 percent of the skin on the boy's back cleared, 50 to 70 percent of the skin on his buttocks, thighs, and legs cleared.

Then there were no further changes. Despite repeated sessions of hypnosis, the boy's fingers and feet remained unchanged, and the still unchanged areas on the back, buttocks, thighs, and legs did not improve. For whatever reason, the treatment had run its course.

Four years later, the young man's skin was the same. The 70 percent of the skin that he had cleared in a small number of hypnosis sessions was still clear. The skin that had not cleared was unchanged.

When Mason wrote up the case for the *British Medical Journal,* the report became the object of widespread interest. (By noon of the day on which it appeared, writes a historian of the episode, "the *Journal* had to open a special switchboard to receive calls from as far away as India.") Over the years, the case continues to be mentioned as an intriguing curiosity, as if it were one of a kind. "Few people seem to be aware," Barber reports, that "Mason's 'unbelievable' results were confirmed by three later investigators."

An English doctor, C. A. S. Wink, who had read Mason's paper, used Mason's hypnotic procedures to treat two young sisters, ages six and eight, who both suffered from fish-skin disease. In six months, "the eight-year-old girl showed from 50 to 75 percent reduction in skin thickness in various areas of the body, and the six-year-old girl showed a 75 percent reduction in skin thickness on the face, and a 20 to 40 percent reduction in skin thickness on other parts of the body."

A Scottish practitioner, C. B. Kidd, used hypnosis to help a 34-year-old man clear away 90 percent of the "fish skin" that covered his body. (The doctor was not able to help the man's 4-year-old son because the boy "was distractible and would not attend to the suggestions.")

A doctor in New York, J. M. Schneck, used hypnosis to help a young woman clear her body of 50 percent of another scale-like skin disease. As with Mason's treatment of the 16-year-old boy, changes came about rapidly—on this occasion, within a week of the first session—and then basically stopped, despite several months of additional sessions.

In a variant of these cases, a trio of American doctors, J. F. Mullins, N. Murray, and E. M. Shapiro, combined hypnosis with psychotherapy to treat a hospitalized 11-year-old boy who suffered from a painful congenital skin disease that affected his soles, palms, knees, elbows, and nails. The boy's fingernails and toenails were "markedly enlarged and extremely hard," his soles and palms were covered with thick and enlarged material, and his elbows and knees were covered with raised red patches of skin. His soles were so tender that "he walked only with crutches, or crawled."

The combined hypnotic and psychotherapeutic treatment consisted of both suggestions that the skin in one or another area of the boy's body would improve and comments encouraging the boy to express and act out aggressive feelings that the doctors had identified in a prior psychological examination. In less than a month, the boy was able to walk without pain. Soon after, his palms showed "dramatic improvement."

117

To Barber, the five studies are "sufficient to topple the dualistic dichotomy between mind and body in Western culture since Descartes." Their meaning, he maintains, is unmistakable. "They show that, in at least some individuals, abnormally functioning skin cells begin to function normally when the individual is exposed to specific words or communications (suggestions)."

Barber surveys many other kinds of cases to document the capacity of "hypnotic (suggestion)" to change the body. Among skin disorders warts are a frequently successful object of treatment by hypnosis, Barber notes. Approximately a dozen studies from Germany, England, and the United States report that substantial percentages of their subjects lost sometimes long-enduring warts after either hypnotic suggestions that the warts would tingle and soon disappear or a placebo drug treatment. (The placebo drug treatment was suggestion given physical form.)

In the instance of skin disorders, the problem "treated" by hypnosis or suggestion already exists. Hypnosis and suggestion can also influence bodily responses to anticipated events. In Japan, two researchers conducted an experiment with 13 young men between the ages of 15 and 17 who had all experienced allergic reactions to a plant similar to poison ivy. After hypnotizing 5 of the subjects and giving "suggestions only" to the other 8, the researchers touched an arm of each subject with a nonpoisonous leaf but told the young men that it was from the poison ivy–like plant to which they were allergic. All 13 subjects, whether hypnotized or in the suggestions-only group, developed the skin rash associated with the poison ivy–like plant.

Then the researchers reversed the experiment. They touched their subjects with a poisonous leaf but said that it was harmless. This time 11 subjects "believed" the doctors. Four of the 5 who were hypnotized and 7 of the 8 from the suggestions-only group—did not develop a skin rash.

"(Hypnotic) suggestion" has been used equally well to prevent the manifestation of any number of already established skin or respiratory allergies.

Some people, through (hypnotic) suggestion, can reproduce wheals or inflammations that they had experienced in the past. With burns at least, the suggestion sometimes does not need to be more than a reminder of the past.

In one case, a doctor, attempting to get a woman patient to relax and be comfortable, hypnotized her and suggested that she imagine herself on a sunny beach. The woman immediately showed signs of distress and cried out, "I feel like I'm on fire." Her face, shoulders, and half of her arms became beet red.

The reaction, a genuine sunburn, lasted 18 hours. The woman, the doctor learned, had once been at the beach and had experienced an allergic reaction to the sun, possibly from a drug she was taking. The doctor's suggestion, under hypnosis, that she see herself on a sunny beach was enough to physically re-create a close approximation of her allergic reaction.

Some people have no need of an actual past experience to evoke precise physical changes in their bodies. The intensity of their imaginations or beliefs are apparently enough. (Barber believes this is especially true of people who are easily hypnotized.) "There are at least fifty well-documented cases of individuals who thought often about and identified with the suffering of Christ," he reports, "and who apparently bled spontaneously and developed skin alterations on their hands or feet which resembled Christ's wounds during his crucifixion."

People under (hypnotic) suggestion can also reduce the loss of blood from certain surgical procedures. In one study, nine people each had the same two teeth pulled from opposite sides of the mouth, a tooth at a time on two separate occasions. The extractions took place under anesthesia, but for one extraction the patients were hypnotized and were given suggestions to reduce the bleeding that would occur.

"They could visualize the blood as water from a faucet that can be turned off, or they could imagine that they were suturing the wound so that it would not bleed, or they could willfully constrict the blood vessels in the area." The patients who received these instructions bled an average of 65% less than they bled during their nonhypnotized extractions.

What else can hypnotic (suggestion) do? In 5 studies, Barber reports, a total of 70 women used (hypnotic) suggestion to increase their breast sizes an average of 1¼ inches in 12 weeks. The women were variously told to imagine warm water flowing over their breasts or warm towels covering them or the sun or a heat lamp shining on them, and to imagine that their breasts "are becoming warm, tingling, pulsating, and that they are growing." They were instructed to give themselves these suggestions in sessions of self-hypnosis at home.

The eventual increase in breast sizes could not be attributed to imprecise measurements or other physiological changes, including weight gain and menstrual cycle. In one of the studies, nearly half of the women lost 2 or more pounds during the 12 weeks.

"Of the many tissues and organs in the human body," Barber asks, pointing to the dramatic possibility that underlies these studies, "which can be altered in size by suggestive psychological approaches?"

Sources of Change: Blood Flow and Credible Suggestions.

What happens in the body when the mind succeeds in changing it? Barber believes that the answer has a great deal to do with blood flow. We all know, he says, that thoughts, feelings, and imaginings can send blood to the sexual organs. Is it not reasonable to suppose that thoughts, feelings, and imaginings can similarly change the blood flow to other tissues and organs of the body?

Biofeedback studies, he points out, have shown that people can increase and decrease the temperature of their fingers and toes by increasing or decreasing the flow of blood to them. (Perhaps the Tibetan monks practicing *gTum-mo* Yoga were calling on some such process.) Studies have also shown that some people can raise or lower the temperature on specific areas of their skin. There are "broad implications" in these findings, Barber believes. "They indicate that we can learn, within a reasonably brief period, to produce substantial changes in blood flow to the periphery of our body, to maintain this changed blood supply over substantial periods of time, and to use this skill for practical purposes, such as keeping warm in a cold climate." (Barber does not note the difference between biofeedback, which operates through a repetitive process of conditioned learning, and hypnosis or suggestion, under which some people have a seemingly immediate capacity to create burns, stop allergic reactions, or clear away diseased skin.)

Once we accept the postulate that blood supply is affected "by cognitions, feelings, imaginings, and other cognitive processes," Barber maintains, it is logical to hypothesize that (hypnotic) suggestions are "incorporated into ongoing cognitions" and that the suggestions then "affect blood supply in localized areas" and help bring about specific physical changes.

If blood flow induces the physical change, what kind of suggestion induces the blood flow? Not all suggestions succeed in changing the body. Barber argues that successful suggestions are "believed-in suggestions" and have a "believed-in efficacy." They are credible. Subjects believe they are realistically possible.

Many factors can contribute to a suggestion's credibility, among them the authority of the people making the suggestions (respected doctors), the setting in which the suggestion is made (a doctor's office), the techniques uses to "activate" the suggestion (hypnosis), and the psychological attitude of the person receiving the suggestion toward the person giving it (as in the identification patients in therapy sometimes feel for their therapists). In some people (who have been burned, for example, or had allergic reactions), past experience can help make suggestions credible.

A number of people also have highly vivid imaginations, and in such people, Barber believes, the imagination usually creates all the credibility that a suggestion needs. Barber says that these people have a "psychosomatic plasticity"—an extreme capacity to turn suggestions about the body into bodily realities—and that they are to be found among the approximately 4 percent of the population who are easily hypnotized.

In an intensive interview study of 29 "highly hypnotizable" women that Barber conducted with Sheryl Wilson, he found that the women had an intense fantasy life and a remarkable capacity to translate their feelings and imaginings into the physical material of their bodies. They were capable of conjuring up at will whole sequences of experiences that often were more real to them, physiologically as well as emotionally, than the physical experiences of their daily lives.

Many of the women had the capacity to bring themselves to orgasm with only their thoughts/fantasies/imaginings. Watching movies, they invariably mimicked in their bodies conditions of physical discomfort. One woman, watching *Dr. Zhivago* on television, became so cold during scenes in which a couple is snowbound in an unheated cottage that she needed to cover herself with blankets. Another woman, watching a movie in which a character drinks beer in a truck while riding over a bumpy road, was unable to get out of the theater before vomiting. In general, the women tended to distract themselves from scenes of violence, to which they otherwise would often react by developing headaches or feelings of nausea.

A striking statistic is that 60% of these women (an extremely high number) had experienced false pregnancies. Not only did they stop menstruating, but they typically had experienced at least four of the following five symptoms: abdominal enlargement, morning sickness, breast changes, cravings for specific foods, and fetal movements. For most of the women, the symptoms disappeared after they learned from medical tests that they were not pregnant. But two of the women, Barber reports, actually underwent abortions.

In the case studies that Barber examines, belief seems to have the capacity (in certain instances, under certain conditions) to create the physical reality of the body.

A Different Kind of Mind

The distinctive feature of most of the people in the studies in Barber's paper is that they deliberately and overtly tell their bodies to do something—get rid of warts, not bleed as much as usual after a tooth extraction, grow larger breasts—and their bodies do it. This is a kind of mind—without quotation marks now—that we have not seen before. All the other "minds" have gone about their business on their own, without, in effect, talking to anyone in charge: They were the entities in charge, if anyone or anything was, moving toward targets that conditions somehow had chosen *for* them. The mind in Barber's article is quite different. It is the kind of mind that we all try to use when we go about making the choices by which we conduct our lives. This is the mind that operates in the light of consciousness (however partial the consciousness may be). This is the kind of mind one can call the "aware mind," and it moves the body too.

The power of the aware mind is that it moves the body deliberately. With the aware mind, there is no accumulating physical wreckage caused by a ceaselessly repeating emotion, no use of a form of concentration that by itself induces a state of calm, no altering of visceral responses through rewards and punishments after the responses have been made "visible" by a machine, no altering of immune responses after they carefully have been associated with other reactions, no automatic orchestration of neuropeptides to their receptors in response to the persistent flow of information into the body. There is instead a desired physical change and a mind that consciously seeks it--and (in some cases, under certain conditions) brings it about.

The "emotional mind," the "mind" that snaps itself into an act of concentration, the "trial-and-error mind," the "conditioned mind," the "neuropeptide mind"--all of them are in our bodies, and we should be thankful that they are. Probably none of us would be alive without them. But Barber's work shows that we also have a mind that we can control, the aware mind, and that we can use it to speak to our bodies directly and intentionally and sometimes make them change.

CHAPTER 7

Gerald Epstein and the Medicine of Imagery

I<small>F</small> the aware mind can move the body, is it possible to use this mind regularly to fix the physical disorders of the body? Is it possible to construct a medicine that is based on the mind?

Gerald Epstein is a psychiatrist in private practice. Epstein uses imagery to cure physical disorders, all physical disorders. A person coming to Epstein with a physical problem (or, for that matter, an emotional problem) is, under most circumstances, given an imagery exercise and told how many times to do the exercise and for how many days. People sometimes create the central image of the exercises for themselves. In either case, the imagery then presumably takes care of the problem. If the illness or the emotional problem is severe, the treatment may include several sessions of a special type of psychotherapy that essentially uses a narrative form of imagery.

Imagery has become an increasingly common element in therapy and even in certain medical situations. In therapy, imagery is used to help people in various ways: to understand what their problems literally look like to them, to illuminate the events that may be involved in the development of the problems, to work through the problems by "working on" the imagery. In medicine, imagery has gained a place in some cancer clinics as a method of moderating the so-called side effects of chemotherapy. Patients are told, in one form or another, to imagine that the chemicals entering their blood are a gentle healing balm.

But in essentially all such uses of imagery, the imagery is part of a larger therapeutic program. For Epstein, the imagery *is* the program. The "prescriptions" he writes are imagery exercises, and he writes them for all physical disorders. In his medicine, the primary and most important method of healing the body is the mind applying images.

Epstein is not averse to prescribing various medications or any needed medical procedures: He believes in relieving symptoms and restoring the body to a healthful state as quickly as possible. But he maintains that under most conditions, the mind, using imagery, can heal all ills and that the mind is the central tool that human beings have to heal their ills. In his perspective, drugs and surgery are, for the most part, not necessary: They often are inadequate, they sometimes complicate a patient's condition, and they occassionally are physically harmful.

The idea that the mind, through imagery, can heal physical disorders—not just a cold but a broken arm, not just a rash or high blood pressure but viral conjunctivitis—is to many people (particularly medical people) a fantasy, possibly a dangerous one. But Epstein's use of the conscious mind to affect the body can be related in many ways to the findings of mind-body research, and in particular to the results described by Theodore Barber in his "New Look at Hypnosis, Cognitions, Imagining, and the Mind-Body Problem."

Epstein is a single practitioner. The results he offers are the stories of his patients, which in the hierarchy of medical evidence ranks as the least trustworthy form of substantiation. (Epstein's results do not stand alone, though. The literature of imagery contains many, often startling instances of practitioners who successfully used imagery to resolve a physical ill.) His work nonetheless offers a dramatic example of what a medicine using the mind might look like.

Epstein's Revelation

Epstein came to his understanding of imagery through what can only be called a revelatory experience that, appropriately enough, centered on an image (maybe all revelatory experiences do).

Epstein had been trained as a psychoanalyst, and he began his private practice in 1972. He had developed an interest in the relation between psychiatry and the law, had co-founded *The Journal of Psychiatry and Law* in 1973 (which he would continue to edit until 1986), and in 1974 he was in Jerusalem as a visiting professor of psychiatry and law. While he was there, he met a young man who described the inability of psychoanalysis to cure him of a severe depression. The young man had gone to an analyst five days a week for three years without relief. Then he had gone to a therapist who practiced something called "waking dream therapy," and in only four sessions, once a week, he was rid of his depression.

As Epstein tells the story in his book *Healing Visualizations,* published in 1989, he found himself "deeply aroused" by this testimony, and he met with the young man's therapist, a woman named Colette Aboulker-Muscat, to learn about her techniques. Aboulker-Muscat explained that her work used imagery to create new perspectives and patterns of living and that it had nothing to do with the sort of interpretive analysis that Freudians applied to nighttime dreams. In the course of the conversation, Epstein told Aboulker-Muscat that Freud had once used an image to help prospective analysts learn how to explain analysis to their patients. Freud had suggested that analysis could be viewed as a train ride during which patients, looking out the windows, reported to their analyst-companions next to them all that they saw and felt.

Aboulker-Muscat responded with an apparent *nonsequitur.* "In what direction does a train go?" Epstein writes that he was "caught short." He wondered if he was being tested. He replied that a train usually went "this way," and made a horizontal gesture with his arm.

"Well," Aboulker-Muscat asked, "what if the direction were changed to this axis?"—and moved her hand and forearm upward. The gesture changed Epstein's life.

> I cannot detail what went through my mind at that moment. I am not sure that I knew then. What I did know, and still know as the truth of that moment, is that I felt an overwhelming sense of self-recognition, what is called an "aha" experience. It was an epiphany. The vertical movement [of Aboulker-Muscat's arm] seemed to lift me from the horizontal hold of the given, the ordinary patterns of everyday cause and effect. I leapt into freedom, and I saw that the task of therapy—the task of being human—was to help realize freedom, to go beyond the given, to the newness that we all are capable of, and to our capacity to renew and re-create.

The shift that Epstein experienced can be described in various ways, perhaps none of which are entirely complete. From the train that moves horizontally—Freud's train—one can see only the details of the present rushing by to become the past. From the train that moves vertically off the earth into the sky—Aboulker-Muscat's train—one sees events that on the earth are variously past, present, and future, but in the air are all present, a single vision. In the contrast, Epstein recognized the possibility of a therapy that treated the present not only in terms of the past but also in terms of an imagined future that could help shape it.

Epstein decided to study with Aboulker-Muscat. As he put it, he became "an apprentice in imagination."

He began introducing imagery into his practice, but found it difficult to merge the approaches of imagery and psychoanalysis. Imagery had the effect of changing behavior by using the imagination to envision new possibilities, and the changes came with relative speed and ease. Psychoanalysis, on the other hand, as Epstein more and more came to see it, was focused primarily on the effort to attribute the present to past "causes," and the changes that occurred came very slowly.

In 1976, Epstein broke with psychoanalysis. In the next several years, he developed an approach to psychotherapy that centrally depended on the use of the imagination and imagery. His largest single influence was Aboulker-Muscat, but he also drew on a number of other European therapists, Jung and Medard Boss among them. He described his approach in a book called *Waking Dream Therapy: Dream Process as Imagination,* published in 1981.

In Epstein's form of waking dream (a technique that some psychotherapies use as an adjunct to the therapeutic process) patients continue the events of their nighttime dreams. They sit with eyes closed and describe the narratives that appear in their imaginations seemingly without effort. With the therapist's guidance, the patients meet, overcome, and resolve the problems that emerge in the narratives. The broad purpose of such waking dreams is to give people the opportunity to move successfully through situations or emotions that daunt them. The premise of Epstein's therapy is that the imagined experience alters the significance of past events and creates new ways to meet experiences yet to happen.

Waking Dream Therapy is about emotional disorders and what might be called life problems—an inability to choose between clear alternatives, writer's block, a lack of purpose, and so forth. But Epstein had also begun to use imagery to treat physical problems, and over the years, he handled an increasing variety of complaints. In 1989, Epstein brought together in *Healing Visualizations: Creating Health Through Imagery* many of the imagery exercises that he, Aboulker–Muscat, or his patients had developed to treat physical disorders. With this book Epstein staked his calm that imagery could heal the body.

Imagery as Treatment for Physical Disorders

Epstein's basic technique of treating a physical disorder with imagery is simple however elaborate the imagery. A person visualizes the disorder and then, still in the imagination, applies a treatment that restores the troubled area to health. The person does this several times a day (usually three times—in the morning, at twilight, and before bed) for a certain number of days or until the disorder disappears. Sometimes the details of the imagery treatment exercise are metaphoric, sometimes they are literal. But the essential strategy is always the same: to use the mind's images, consciously evoked and directed, to resolve a physical problem in the body.

Every exercise is performed with the eyes closed and is introduced by a short breathing exercise: a long breath out through the mouth, a short breath in through the nose, another long breath out and short breath in, and a third long breath out. Out-in breathing quiets the body, Epstein explains; in-out breathing excites it.

The person then inwardly states the purpose of the imagery exercise. Epstein calls the purpose the "intention," whose aim is to set "an inner direction." It is a "kind of computer program" that focuses the mind on the bodily problem the person is trying to resolve. In *Healing Visualizations,* he lists an intention for each exercise, but he explains that the person doing the exercise is the true authority for formulating an intention. "Any intention you give yourself," Epstein declares, "is correct."

Epstein's imagery exercise for warts is representative. Epstein calls the exercise "Reverse Face." (He names all his exercises, sometimes comically. He calls an exercise for hemorrhoids "The Puckered Purse.") The listed intention of the exercise is "To remove warts" or "To heal the skin." (All the exercises described in this chapter come from *Healing Visualizations.*)

> Close your eyes. Breathe out three times [Epstein's phrase for his out-in breathing exercise], and find yourself at a cool, crystal-clear, fresh-flowing mountain stream (or any healing body of water). See your face there (or the part with the warts) and then remove it, turn it inside out, and wash it thoroughly in the stream. See all the waste products as black or gray strands being carried away in the fast-flowing stream with its spiral currents. After your face (or other body part) is thoroughly washed, hang it out to dry in the sun. See it healing from the inside, looking like all the other healthy tissue around it. Then turn the face right side out and put it back in place, seeing that the warts have disappeared. Then open your eyes.

The exercise is to be performed four times a day, for one to three minutes, for three weeks. If the warts do not clear up in that time, the person is to stop doing the exercise for a week and then start again for another three-week period. (The pattern of doing an exercise for three weeks and then stopping for a week is frequent in Epstein's exercises.)

The exercise to relieve the eye disorder of glaucoma, "The Canal of Schlemm," is more literal, and deals so concretely with mechanisms of the eye that Epstein provides an appropriate cross-section drawing. He recommends that anyone doing the exercise examine the drawing for help in visualizing the exercise's imagery.

In glaucoma, the aqueous fluid around the lens of the eye, which normally drains through a duct called the Canal of Schlemm, is not draining properly. The result is a buildup of pressure, which can reduce a person's vision and in some cases lead to blindness. Epstein prescribes the following exercise:

> Close your eyes. Breathe out three times and sense air coming in through the pupil of your eye. As you breathe in, the pupil opens, lets air in, and as you breathe out, the pupil closes. Sense the air creating a ripple in the fluid, and pushing the river of aqueous fluid through the Canal of Schlemm. Feel the wave of fluid flowing through the canal into the adjacent venous sinus (opening), and carrying the fluid away into the venous drainage system of the body. Know that your ocular pressure has returned to normal. Then open your eyes.

The exercise is to be done three times a day, for one to three minutes each time, for three weeks. "Then use the exercise once a day," Epstein writes, "until you have the situation well in hand."

One of the most elaborate exercises in *Healing Visualizations* treats the immune disorder of mononucleosis. The exercise is a trilogy of exercises, each one of which deals with a different aspect of the recovery process. The first aims at ridding the body of the physical source of the problem. The second aims at repairing the damage that has been done to the immune system. The third aims at enhancing the capacities of the immune system. Each exercise is to be done once a day, for three minutes, for a week, the whole set to be completed in three weeks.

Epstein calls the first exercise "The White Knights." White

blood cells perform the immune functions, and the white knights of the exercise are clearly meant to be the white cells of the immune system.

> Close your eyes. Breathe out three times. The white knights have to fight an army of warriors occupying a fortified place. After pushing out the warriors, the knights must fight them off once again during a counterattack the warriors mount in an effort to retake the fort. Then open your eyes.

The second exercise, for the second week, is "The Intimate Defender." At this point in the imagery treatment, the body presumably is free of the warriors that have been attacking it, and the damage they caused now needs to be repaired.

> Close your eyes. Breathe out three times. See the white spots of a leopard's skin. See yourself entering the skin of the great, white-spotted leopard; your hands and feet are completely covered by the skin. See, sense, repair, and put in perfect order all the white spots that are not perfect. Make them all perfectly white and round by planting white hair all around to make a perfect form. When your leopard skin is perfect, feel yourself perfectly well and emerge from it slowly. Then open your eyes.

The third exercise, for the third week, is "The White Eagle." The imagery now depicts actions that are bolder and more ferocious, efforts to build and feed the strength of the body.

> Close your eyes. Breathe out three times. Be a white eagle in the sky. Spot a movement on the ground and know that it is a jaguar. Swoop down and kill the young jaguar and fly back to your nest with it as food for your eaglets. Then spot two young jaguars on the ground. Swoop down, and with each talon take the jaguars back to the nest. Then open your eyes.

Imagery Case Studies

Do such exercises work? Epstein explaines that all the exercises in *Healing Vizualizations* have been used successfully by his patients to resolve physical problems. By way of evidence, he includes a variety of short case histories.

One man who used "The Canal of Schlemm," Epstein reports, had been suffering from glaucoma for nearly eight years when he came to Epstein. An ophthalmologist regularly monitored the pressure on the eye, and the man was taking three medications to maintain the pressure within normal limits.

When people do an imagery exercise, Epstein prefers that they stop taking any medications, but it is not a precondition. Imagery works best, Epstein maintains, when the body is not being influenced by drugs. In this case, the man sought permission from his ophthalmologist to stop the three prescribed medications for a period of three weeks, the length of time he would be doing the glaucoma exercise. The ophthalmologist, although somewhat uncomfortable, agreed, and the man began performing "The Canal of Schlemm" three times a day, as prescribed.

At the end of the three-week period, he returned to his ophthalmologist for another monitoring of eye pressure. Epstein reports that this time, although the man had stopped his medication entirely, the eye pressure, which for eight years had to be constrained by medication, was normal.

Five years later, the man was still practicing "The Canal of Schlemm" exercise and, because the pressure was somewhat above normal, was also taking one medication.

The most remarkable of Epstein's case histories deal with disorders that seem immeasurably beyond the reach of imagery. It is theoretically conceivable that imagery could deal with disorders that are recognized to be psychosomatic— warts, for example. In these instances, a psychological technique is being employed to treat a disorder that may be essentially psychological in nature. But how could one maintain that imagery can successfully treat such disorders as an enlarged prostate, an improperly positioned fetus, or a broken bone, disorders that involve the basic structure and anatomy of a body? Epstein says it can.

The prostate is a gland at the base of a man's bladder. It surrounds the urethra, the passageway for urine and, during ejaculation, semen. In middle-aged men, the prostate often becomes enlarged, causing difficulties with urination and sometimes the release of semen as well. The only recognized medical treatment is surgery. Epstein calls his exercise for prostate enlargement "The Golden Net."

> Close your eyes. Breathe out three times and see yourself entering your body by any opening you choose and finding your prostate. When you have done this, examine it from every angle. Then see yourself placing a thin golden net encircling the prostate. The net has a drawstring that you must pull around your prostate as tightly as you can stand, as you see the gland reducing to its normal size. Then, using your other hand, gently massage the prostate, sensing the seminal fluid and/or urine flowing smoothly and evenly through the neck of the bladder into the urethra, and down the urethra to the tip of the penis, from which you can see the fluid flowing in a stream into the earth, at the same time seeing your prostate shrinking to its normal size. Then open your eyes.

One of the men Epstein treated for an enlarged prostate was in his fifties. He was having trouble both retaining his urine and initiating a normal release of urine. His doctor had told him that the only way he could be relieved of these difficulties was to undergo an operation to reduce the prostate.

An enlarged prostate usually does not require immediate

attention. It is troublesome and distressing but, for the most part, not fundamentally incapacitating. In this case, the man chose to hold off on the operation, and for the next six months (in six cycles of four weeks in which he performed the exercise for three weeks and stopped for one), the man applied the imagery of "The Golden Net." Epstein explains that at the end of six months, the man had stopped having urinary problems. He returned to his doctor, who found that the prostate was now a normal size and no longer required an operation. Two years later, the man's prostate was continuing to function normally.

Imagery, according to Epstein, can also rotate an improperly positioned fetus. Two women who individually had been seeing Epstein for psychotherapeutic reasons each came to him in the eighth month of her pregnancy. Each had been told by her doctor that her fetus had assumed what is called a breech position, with its feet and buttocks rather than its head closest to the cervix, making the baby's delivery more difficult. Breech babies are normally delivered (in the United States, at least) by a cesarian section.

To each woman Epstein prescribed an imagery exercise with the straightforward name "Turning the Fetus."

Close your eyes. Breathe out three times and enter your body by any opening you choose. Carrying a light with you, find your way to your uterus; *carefully* enter your uterus through the cervix, and find the fetus. Then *carefully* and *very gently* turn the fetus to the proper position, with the head facing down toward the birth canal. Note the sensations, if any, that you experience upon doing so. A sensation of pain, if you have one, will tell you that you are succeeding. Then leave the body by *exactly the way you entered*— back through the uterus and cervix, and out of your body by the entry route. When you are outside of your body, breathe out once and open your eyes. On the next succeeding three days, go back to your uterus and check it to see, imaginally, whether the version [the medical term for the turning of the fetus] has taken place. Within a week of the exercise, return to your doctor for an examination. If the fetus hasn't turned to the proper delivery position, try the exercise once again—with more conviction this time.

In both women, the fetuses assumed the normal head-first position—an altogether unlikely occurrence in the eighth month of pregnancy—and each had a normal delivery.

In another case, Epstein reports that imagery helped heal a broken bone in a fourth of the usual time. A woman broke her wrist, and the orthopedist who set it told her that the broken bone was one of the slowest healing bones of the body and would take three months to heal. The woman was in the midst of a business trip between the East and West Coasts, and was seeing two doctors. The second orthopedist confirmed the diagnosis that the bone would take three months to heal.

Epstein recommended that the woman help the healing process with an imagery exercise called "Weaving the Marrow."

Close your eyes. Breathe out three times and see the ends of the bones as they now look. See the two ends touching each other. See and sense the marrow flowing from one end into the other. See this white marrow carried in blue channels of lights flowing through the red bloodstream, seeing the arterioles flowing back and forth between the two ends, forming a woven net that brings the two ends closer. See the two ends knitting together perfectly until you can no longer see any sign of a break. Know that the bone is now one, and open your eyes.

After three weeks the woman felt that the bone had knitted back together. She had been performing the exercise every three or four hours (while she was awake) for approximately three minutes each time. When the original orthopedist removed the cast at the woman's insistence and found that the wrist had indeed healed, he was so disconcerted that he immediately reviewed the woman's x-rays and confirmed that the broken bone had been the one that regularly took three months to heal.

Imagery and the Other Mind-Body Connections

What is one to make of all this? How can one credit it? Epstein's work appears to be far outside the normal understandings of biological medicine, even far outside the perspectives of most researchers investigating the mind's influence on the body.

In fact, a web of similarities and parallels connects Epstein's work to many mind-body findings. The case studies reported by Theodore Barber provide the most obvious link. In cases like the young man with fish-skin disease—who rid himself of 70 percent of his skin disturbance through hypnosis—and the Japanese adolescents who, through hypnosis or suggestion, physiologically responded to a poisonous leaf as if it had no toxic properties and to a nontoxic leaf as if it were poisonous—it is clear that somewhere in the mind is the capacity, pure and simple, to direct the body to do its bidding. Epstein's work employs this capacity and uses imagery to call upon it.

There may be other ways to call upon this capacity, but imagery is Epstein's way, and it is clear that imagery is involved in many of Barber's cases.

The patient with fish-skin disease was told to focus on a particular part of his body and imagine the skin clearing up. He used his imagination to restore his skin to health. What went through the minds of the Japanese adolescents is unknown, but it is not unreasonable to suppose that they pictured being touched by either poisonous or benign leaves.

138

The 70 women, in five studies, who succeeded in increasing their breast sizes an average of 1¼ inches used imagery. They were told to imagine warm water flowing over their breasts or warm towels covering them or the sun or a heat lamp shining on them. Such images are perhaps more pedestrian than the images of Epstein's exercises—less imaginative—but they are images.

Is it not possible to move from these studies to the case history of the man who succeeded in bringing his enlarged prostate back to normal size? Barber asked the question: "Of the many tissues and organs in the human body, which can be altered in size by suggestive psychological approaches?" If women can enlarge their breasts through imagery, why might a man not be able to reduce his prostate the same way?

And if imagery can do these things, why might it not be possible for imagery to change the position of a fetus? The situations on the surface appear different. With breasts and the prostate gland, a single organ is involved, and the imagery presumably works on the cells of the organ. To move a fetus means taking an anatomical structure that is pointed one way and somehow physically rotating it. It is hard even to identify the bodily processes that might be involved in such a rotation, which seems to be a matter of lifting an object and turning it around with one's hands. But if breast and prostate glands can be altered, why can't fetuses be turned? Where does the line between possible and impossible fall?

There are other overlaps with other researchers. The Tibetan monks studied by Herbert Benson strikingly increased the temperature of their bodies. In the *gTum-mo* Yoga that the monks practiced, they imagined—imaged—a fire in their bodies. Did this imaging contribute to the temperature increases? (If the monks had imagined being frozen in a block of ice would their temperatures still have gone up?) If images can increase temperature, why might they not move the aqueous fluid around the lens of an eye?

Robert Ader demonstrated that rats can be conditioned to alter an immune reaction as part of a response to a neutral stimulus. The rats do the altering, not the stimulus. Epstein says that humans can rid themselves of an immune disorder like mononucleosis by using imagery. Ader has shown with rats that the immune system can be influenced by what the mind (the brain, the central nervous system) knows. Is it unreasonable to suppose that what rats can be taught to do involuntarily, humans might be able to do voluntarily?

None of these similarities or overlaps or possible connections proves that images can move biological processes virtually at will. But they show that such a possibility is in principle no more outlandish and improbable than, say, the possibility that the brain can dictate to the immune system.

The Power of the Mind

An important feature of Epstein's work is his contention, demonstrated in the examples from *Healing Visualizations*, that once a physical disorder appears, the mind, through imagery, can go to work on it without an investigation of "causes," most particularly, "psychological causes." (Epstein would substitute "emotional and social" for "psychological.")

Epstein believes that emotions and social relationships do play an integral part in the development of many physical disorders. In fact, he maintains that there are clear associations between certain illnesses and particular emotional and social imbalances. "With most eye problems," he claims, "the emotional/social issue of what it is we don't want to see, or what we have been blind to, has to be taken into account." Coronary problems, he maintains, "always involve troubles with love." Disturbances of the pancreas may involve "cruelty directed either against ourselves or against someone else." People may come to feel the need to examine the emo-

tional and social components of their illnesses. Sometimes, details and events that occur while doing an imagery exercise will illuminate such components and will lead people to make changes in their lives. Describing the case of the man with an enlarged prostate, Epstein cryptically notes that "in the course of the treatment," the man "very quickly was able to identify an important problematic area in his life that he related to his malfunctioning prostate" and was able to correct it.

But people do not need to dig for reasons and causes before they can successfully apply imagery. Imagery produces its physical effects, according to Epstein, because of the imagery: What happens in the mind, he believes, happens in the body. Why the body develops its disorder is one issue; treating the disorder is another.

The women who increased the size of their breasts are proof of Epstein's contention. The women did not investigate why, from the viewpoint of their feelings and attitudes, they might have had small breasts or why they were unhappy with the size of their breasts. They simply imagined their breasts being covered and filled with warmth and then imagined them tingling and growing.

Epstein's work shows that a medicine that uses the mind does not have to be a medicine that depends on an elaborate psychologizing of illness. An illness may or may not have emotional and social components. But the mind is more than emotions and feelings, and has its own powers. Through biofeedback, which obviously does not depend on emotions, people can be taught to affect their blood pressure and the temperature of their bodies. Rats, whatever their emotions or relationships, can be taught to control certain immune reactions. Women can enlarge their breasts by imagining them becoming warm and growing. People having teeth extracted can use images to reduce their bleeding. And, according to Epstein, people can speed up the healing of broken bones by applying an imagery exercise called "Weaving the Marrow," and can treat any other disorder of the body by similarly repairing or correcting it in their minds.

The Close of the Investigation, But Not the End

Epstein's work brings this investigation of mind-body studies to a close. Several points should be clear: Emotions are not the only way the mind can affect the body. The mind (the brain, the central nervous system) can be trained to alter specific responses and processes of the body. No system in the body is autonomous and closed off to the influence of the mind. The mind, under certain conditions, can consciously ask the body to change and the body will comply. It also seems clear that no view of the mind that derives from studies on animals—creatures without self-consciousness—can explain the capacity of human beings to directly influence their bodies. The rat that does what it does because of conditioning—how can this explain the young man who cleared away 70 percent of his "incurable" fish–skin disease?

One last point is more problematic and depends on whether one believes in the mind and not just the "mind": No medicine that comprehensively seeks to treat the ills of the body with the mind is possible without an aware mind—a mind that makes its own choices.

Reading List

THIS list consists of the articles and books that I drew on most directly in my research. I also want to mention Caleb Gattegno's *The Mind Teaches the Brain,* a little-known monograph that has been an important influence on my thinking. Gattegno was an extraordinary educator whose analysis of learning led him to a rich (if difficult and idiocyncratic) study of the guiding role of the mind in an individual's unceasing encounters with life. *The Mind Teaches the Brain* is available from Educational Solutions, 95 University Place, New York, N.Y. 10003.

Introduction

Barber, Theodore X. "Changing 'Unchangeable' Bodily Processes by (Hypnotic) Suggestions: A New Look at Hypnosis, Cognitions, Imagining, and the Mind-Body Problem." In *Imagination and Healing,* edited by Anees A. Sheikh. Baywood Publishing Co., Farmingdale, New York, 1984.

The *New England Journal of Medicine* editorial attacking mind–body research (written by Marcia Angell) appeared on June 13,

143

1985 (vol. 312, no. 24); the *Journal of the American Medical Association* attacking the germ theory appeared almost exactly 100 years earlier, on July 12, 1884.

Chapter 1.

Case, Robert B., Stanley, S. Heller, Nan B. Case, Arthur J. Moss, et al. "Type A Behavior and Survival After Acute Myocardial Infarction." *New England Journal of Medicine,* June 13, 1985 (vol. 312, no. 24).

Fischman, Joshua. "Type A on Trial." *Psychology Today,* February 1987.

Friedman, Meyer and Ray H. Rosenman. *Type A Behavior and Your Heart.* Knopf, New York, 1974.

Friedman, Meyer, Carl E. Thoresen, et al. "Alteration of Type A Behavior and Its Effects on Cardiac Recurrence in Post Myocardial Infarction Patients: Summary Results of the Recurrent Coronary Prevention Project." *American Heart Journal,* October 1986 (vol. 112, n. 4).

Friedman, Meyer and Diana Ulmer. *Treating Type A and Your Heart.* Knopf, New York, 1984.

Ragland, David R., and Richard J. Brand. "Type A Behavior and Mortality from Coronary Heart Disease." *New England Journal of Medicine,* January 14, 1988 (vol. 318, no. 2).

Rosenman, Ray H. "History and Definition of the Type A Coronary-Prone Behavior Pattern." In *Coronary-Prone Behavior,* edited by Theodore M. Dembroski, et al. Spring-Verlag, New York, 1978.

———, Richard J. Brand, et al. "Coronary Heart Disease in the Western Collaborative Group Study." *Journal of the American Medical Association,* July 6, 1964 (vol. 189, no. 1).

———, Meyer Firedman, et al. "A Predictive Study of Coronary Heart Disease." *Journal of the American Medical Association,* July 6, 1964 (vol. 189, no. 1).

Williams, Redford. *The Trusting Heart.* Times Books, New York, 1989.

Chapter 2.

Benson, Herbert. "Your Innate Asset for Combatting Stress." *Harvard Business Review,* 1974 (vol. 52).

———. *The Relaxation Response.* William Morrow, New York, 1975.

———. *Beyond the Relaxation Response.* Times Books, New York, 1984.

———. *Your Maximum Mind.* Random House, New York, 1987.

———, F. Beary, and M. P. Carol. "The Relaxation Response." *Psychiatry,* February 1974 (vol. 37).

———, et al. "Body Temperature Changes During the Practice of gTummo (Heat) Yoga." *Nature,* June 23, 1982 (vol. 295).

———, J. A. Herd, W. H. Morse, and R. T. Kelleher. "Behavioral Induction of Hypertension in the Squirrel Monkey." *American Journal of Physiology,* 1969 (vol. 217).

———, B. A. Rosner, B. A. Marzetts, and H. Klemchuk. "Decreased Blood Pressure in Pharmacologically Treated Hypertensive Patients Who Regularly Elicited the Relaxation Response." *The Lancet,* February 23, 1974 (vol. 289).

Eisenberg, David. *Encounters with Qi.* Norton, New York, 1985.

Wallace, R. Keith and Herbert Benson. "The Physiology of Meditation." *Scientific American,* February 1972 (vol 84).

Chapter 3.

Birk, Lee. "Introduction." In *Biofeedback: Behavior Medicine,* edited by Birk. Grune & Stratton, New York, 1973.

Brucker, Bernard S., and Laurence P. Ince. "Biofeedback as an Experimental Treatment for Postural Hypotension in a Patient with Spinal Cord Lesion." In *Biofeedback and Self-Control, 1977/78,* edited by Johann Stoyva, et al. Aldine, Chicago, 1978.

Lynch, James J. "Furor Therapeuticus Revisited." In *Biofeedback: Behavioral Medicine,* edited by Lee Birk. Grune & Stratton, New York, 1973.

Jonas, Gerald. *Visceral Learning.* Viking Press, New York, 1973.

Miller, Neal E. "Integration of Neurophysical and Behavioral Research." *Annals of New York Academy of Sciences,* 1961 (vol. 92).

———. "Learning of Visceral and Glandular Responses." *Science,* January 31, 1969 (vol. 163).

———. "Interaction Between Learned and Physical Factors in Mental Illness." *Seminars in Psychiatry,* August 1972 (vol. 4, no. 3).

———. "Biofeedback and Visceral Learning." *Annual Review of Psychology,* 1978 (vol. 29).

———, and Bernard S. Brucker. "Learned Large Increases in Blood Pressure Apparently Independent of Skeletal Response in Patients Paralyzed by Spinal Lesions." In *Biofeedback and Self-Regulation,* edited by Neils Birbaumer and H. D. Kimmel. Erlbaum Assoc., Hillsdale, N.J., 1979.

———, and Barry Dworkin. "Visceral Learning: Recent Difficulties with Curarized Rats and Significant Problems for Human Research." In *Biofeedback and Self-Control, 1974,* edited by Leo V. DiCara, et al. Aldine, Chicago, 1975.

Chapter 4.

Ader, Robert. "Experimentally Induced Gastric Lesions: Results and Implications of Studies in Animals." In *Duodenal Ulcer,* edited by Herbert Weiner. Karger, Basel, Switzerland, 1971.

———, editor. *Psychoneuroimmunology.* Academic Press, New York, 1981.

———. "The Placebo Effect as a Conditioned Response." In *Experimental Foundations of Behavioral Medicine: Conditioning Approaches,* edited by Robert Ader, Herbert Weiner, and Andrew Baum. Erlbaum, Hillsdale, N.J., 1988.

Chapter 5.

Ruff, Michael, and Candace B. Pert. "Neuropeptides Are Chemoat-
tractants for Human Monocytes and Tumor Cells: A Basis for
Mind-Body Communication." In *Enkephalins and Endorphins
Stress and the Immune System,* edited by Nicholas P. Plotnikoff,
et al. Plenum Publishing Corporation, New York, 1986.

Pert, Candace B. "The Wisdom of the Receptors." *Advances,* Sum-
mer 1986 (vol. 3, no. 3). A slightly edited version of this paper
appeared in *Noetic Sciences Review,* Spring 1987. Institute of
Noetic Sciences, 475 Gate Road, Sausalito, California 94965.

———, with Harris Dienstfrey. "The Neuropeptide Network." *Annals of New York Academy of Science,* 1988 (vol. 521).

———, and Solomon H. Snyder. "Opiate Receptor: Demonstration
in Nervous Tissue." *Science,* March 9, 1973 (vol. 179).

———, et al. "Neuropeptides and Their Receptors: A Psychosomatic
Network." *Journal of Immunology,* August 1985 (vol. 135, no. 2).

Snyder, Solomon H. *Brainstorming: The Science and Politics of
Opiate Research.* Harvard University Press, Cambridge, Mass.,
1989.

Chapter 6.

Barber, Theodore X. "Changing 'Unchangeable' Bodily Processes
by (Hypnotic) Suggestions: A New Look at Hypnosis, Cognitions,
Imagining, and the Mind-Body Problem." In *Imagination and
Healing,* edited by Anees A. Sheikh. Baywood Publishing Co.,
Farmingdale, New York, 1984.

———, and Sheryl C. Wilson. "Hypnosis, Suggestions, and Altered
States of Consciousness: Experimental Evaluation of the New
Cognition-Behavioral Theory and the Traditional Trance-State
Theory of 'Hypnosis.'" In *Biofeedback and Self-Control, 1977/78,*
edited by Johann Stoyva et al. Aldine, Chicago, 1978.

Spanos, Nicholas P., and John F. Chaves. "Hypnosis Research: A
Methodological Critique of Experiments Generated by Two Alter-

native Paradigms." *American Journal of Clinical Hypnosis,* 1970 (vol. 13).

Wilson, Sheryl C., and Theodore X. Barber. "The Fantasy-Prone Personality: Implications for Understanding Imagery, Hypnosis, and Parapsychological Phenomena." In *Imagery: Curent Theory, Research and Application,* edited by Anees A. Sheikh. John Wiley, New York, 1983.

Chapter 7.

Epstein, Gerald. *Waking Dream Therapy: Dream Process as Imagination.* Human Sciences Press, New York, 1981.

———. *Healing Visualizations: Creating Health Through Imagery.* Bantam Books, New York, 1989.

INDEX